The NEW SPANISH

Jonah MILLER   Nate ADLER

The NEW SPANISH

BiTES, FEASTS, AND DRiNKS

KYLE BOOKS

Published in 2018 by Kyle Books
www.kylebooks.com

Distributed by National Book Network
4501 Forbes Blvd, Suite 200,
Lanham, MD 20706
Phone: (800) 462-6420
Fax: (800) 338-4550
customercare@nbnbooks.com

10 9 8 7 6 5 4 3 2 1

ISBN: 978-1-909487-83-3

Project Editor: Christopher Steighner
Designer: Phil Wong
Photographer: Ramsay de Give
Illustrator: Hugo Yoshikawa
Production: Nic Jones, Gemma John, and Lisa Pinnell

Library of Congress Control Number: 2017963600

Color reproduction by ALTA London
Printed and bound in China by 1010 International Printing Ltd.

IT ALL STARTED WITH THE ROTOS.

Huevos rotos, the classic way, is a big mess of french fries, hunks of chorizo, and fried eggs (*rotos* means "broken" or "crashed"—everything just tossed together on a plate). It's a greasy-spoon dish in Spain, as old school as corned beef hash or sloppy joes in the U.S. It was a dish we loved, but we wanted to take it from a Spanish truck stop to downtown Manhattan. We made *huevos rotos* our way.

Instead of french fries, we fried spiralized potatoes, spooned chorizo vinaigrette over the delicate but crunchy strands, and slid a slow-poached egg on top. We let the diner break the egg over the potatoes so that the yolk and chorizo made a rich, delicious sauce. With that, the most-talked-about dish at Huertas, our restaurant, was born.

This dish encapsulates our approach to Spanish cuisine. We start with a satisfying classic, but using influences from the food mecca that is New York City—a dish at a popular Szechuan spot; a general craze for ramen; personal experience on a bustling pasta station cooking countless bowls of spaghetti carbonara; and a turning slicer, an inexpensive kitchen gadget—we create a dish that's all ours.

Like the *rotos*, it is new takes on Spanish classics that we want to share with home cooks around the country. We believe that Spanish food has never received the same treatment that many other cuisines have in this country—which is to say, our talented, trained, farmers' market–driven chefs haven't really adapted the cooking of Spain to fit the way we eat today. Think of how many chefs have taken tradition and inspiration from Italy, but rather than copying purely Italian food, they created a new Italian-American cuisine that satisfied the American palate. This way of cooking was truly unique and accessible, and as a result can now be found in every corner of the country. That is our approach to Spanish food at Huertas and the idea behind this book: through these recipes, we have striven to create a new Spanish cuisine.

Working in some of New York's finest kitchens as a teenager, Jonah was struck by the groundbreaking cooking happening across the Atlantic at places like Arzak, El Bulli, and Mugaritz. While studying food culture at New York University, he jumped at the chance to spend a semester in Madrid. Living on the famed Calle de las Huertas, it wasn't the laboratory-like modern kitchens that were a revelation, but rather the celebratory and communal nature of the everyday dining.

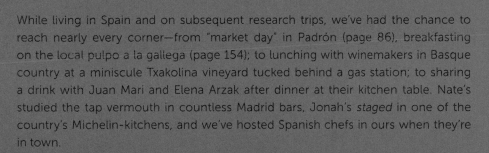

While living in Spain and on subsequent research trips, we've had the chance to reach nearly every corner—from "market day" in Padrón (page 86), breakfasting on the local pulpo a la gallega (page 154); to lunching with winemakers in Basque country at a miniscule Txakolina vineyard tucked behind a gas station; to sharing a drink with Juan Mari and Elena Arzak after dinner at their kitchen table. Nate's studied the tap vermouth in countless Madrid bars, Jonah's *staged* in one of the country's Michelin-kitchens, and we've hosted Spanish chefs in ours when they're in town.

While we look to Spain for inspiration, for the sights and the smells of the festival culture, our job is really to be interpreters and translators. Just because Spaniards love a particular dish classically prepared does not mean it can or should be served unchanged to our guests. In fact, without evolution, many dishes are not met with the same enthusiasm abroad. We spent our first years feverishly changing the menu. Huertas became a laboratory for tweaking classics and treating our seasonal farmers' market produce in ways that relate back to Spain. We've served hundreds of different dishes, and many have evolved countless times along the way. The recipes in *The New Spanish* are battle-tested hits—thousands of guests have enjoyed them, and if they didn't, we were sure to take note and recalibrate accordingly.

In America, we are increasingly eating like Spaniards. We are no longer satisfied by an appetizer, entrée, and dessert. We want to try a bit of this, a bit of that. We want to share with the friends and family that we're gathered with. There aren't any rules for how to combine the recipes in the following chapters. You could host a cocktail party and solely serve *pintxos*. Or have a few friends over for brunch and offer them a *pintxo* when they arrive, followed by an egg dish and a couple of vegetable recipes that match the season. You could throw a birthday party with a single rice dish playing the starring role and a handful of *conservas*, purchased or homemade, as sides. Invite friends for a backyard barbecue—grill a leg of lamb and serve it up with a salad, a loaf of bread, and a trio of any of the sauces you'll come across in the following pages. If it's date night and she loves duck or he adores scallops, make one of those the highlight, serving an egg dish before and some cheese or dessert after.

In *The New Spanish*, you'll find our approach to recognizable classics like Tortilla Española (page 52) and Gambas al Ajillo (page 148); our reincarnations of forgotten favorites like Koskera (page 158) and Zurrukatuna (page 167); and playful dishes like Arroz al Chino (page 106) and our Basque Dog (page 144), which are more New York with a Spanish twist than the other way around. To wash it all down, we've developed Spanish-inspired cocktails, despite the fact that Spaniards are typically not really cocktail drinkers. We mixed up the spirits and fortified wines most popular in Spain with our housemade vermouths to create a unique selection for our menu of *cócteles*. We included the recipes for making our seasonal vermouths and an array of simple syrups in the Drinks chapter (pages 190 to 215)—all easy enough to make at home and use to create, literally, your own "house" Manhattans, martinis, and gin and tonics.

Intrigued by the modernist cooking that has catapulted Spanish chefs onto the world stage, diners around the globe have discovered not just innovation in Spain, but also generations of great cooking that have long been underappreciated. Armed with our updates to a legendary cuisine, your adventures in cooking Spanish bites, feasts, and drinks are just a page turn away.

"MARKET-DRIVEN CHEFS HAVEN'T REALLY ADAPTED THE COOKING OF SPAIN TO FIT THE WAY WE EAT TODAY."

PINTXOS

Gildas White Anchovy, Pickled Pepper, and Manzanilla Olive	16
"Black Gildas" Cured Anchovy, Piquillo Pepper, and Garlic Confit	18
Sardinas y Rábanos Sardines and Radishes	19
Ensaladilla Rusa con Atún Russian Salad with Tuna	20
Ensalada de Huevos y Camarones Egg Salad and Shrimp Toasts	21
Banderillas Mixed Pickle Skewers	23
Rollos de Pepino con Trucha Trout Salad in Cucumber Rolls	24
Piquillos Rellenos Peppers Stuffed with Goat Cheese and Catalan Greens	25
Croquetas de Garbanzos Chickpea Croquettes with Olive Aïoli	26
Croquetas de Pato Duck Croquettes	28
Manchego con Membrillo Manchego and Quince Paste Toasts	30

STEP INTO A PINTXO BAR in Spain and you're surrounded. Imposing

legs of *jamón* hang over your head; cigarette butts, mussel shells, and soiled cocktail napkins dot the floor; conversations buzz in every corner. And then your eyes settle on the prize—the bar lined with countless pintxos, each more tempting than the last.

We like to simply describe pintxos (or pinchos) as "Basque bites." From the verb *pinchar,* meaning "to puncture" or, more apt in the food context, "to skewer," pintxos are traditionally served with a toothpick holding the components together. Their one- or two-bite size makes them comparable to Chinese dim sum or French hors d'oeuvres. Unlike tapas, these items are not intended be shared; rather, each guest can mix and match bites to individual taste. They represent one of the things that we love most about dining in Spain: that there is not much thought involved—no decoding a menu, or deciding how much to order soon after sitting down. Instead, if something looks good, point to it, and seconds later: instant gratification.

While enough pintxos can certainly make up a meal on their own, they are the perfect way to start a dinner or dazzle a crowd during a cocktail party.

EGG SALAD
AND SHRIMP
(21)

DUCK
CROQUETTES
(28)

BLACK
GILDA
(18)

GILDAS
(17)

BANDERILLA
(23)

CHICKPEA CROQUETTE (26)

SMOKED TROUT SALAD (24)

RUSSIAN SALAD WITH TUNA (20)

STUFFED PIQUILLO (25)

SARDINE AND RADISH (19)

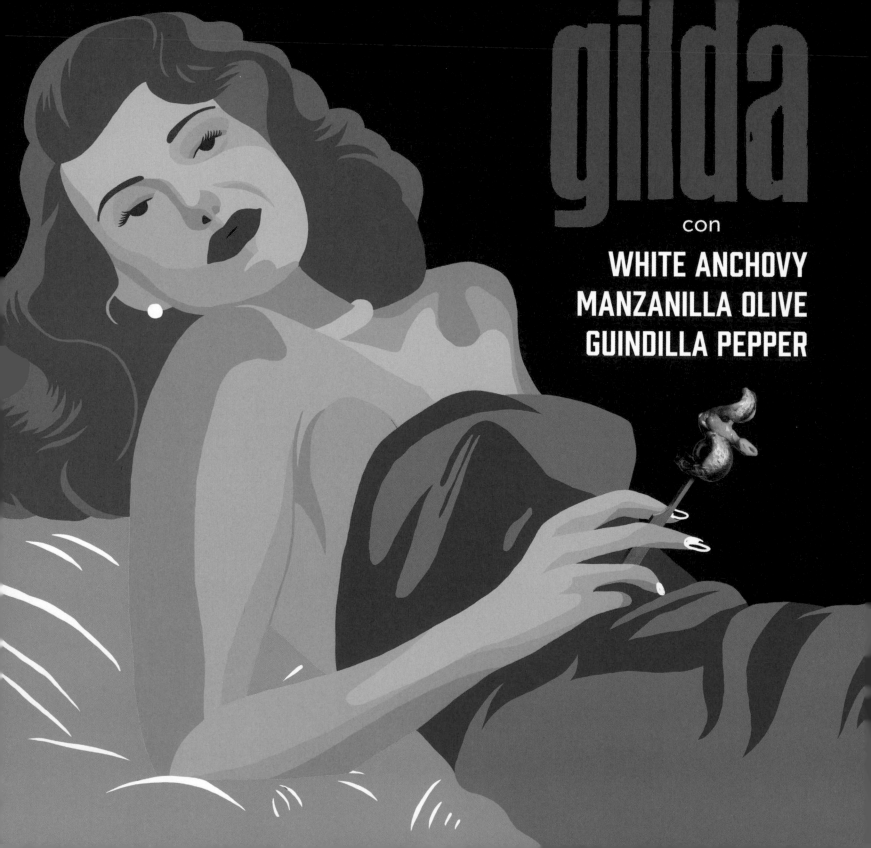

gilda

con

WHITE ANCHOVY
MANZANILLA OLIVE
GUINDILLA PEPPER

THIS IS THE PLACE TO START. NO NEED TO LOOK AT THE MENU. IT ALMOST DOESN'T EVEN MATTER WHAT YOU'RE DRINKING. HAVE A GILDA. HAVE TWO. AMONG THE DIZZYING ARRAY OF PINTXOS LINING THE BARS IN SPAIN, THERE IS ONLY ONE TRUE KING—WELL, QUEEN, REALLY: THE GILDA.

THIS IS THE ONLY PINTXO THAT WE HAVE SERVED EVERY NIGHT SINCE THE DAY WE OPENED, AND WE WILL SERVE IT EVERY NIGHT UNTIL THE DAY WE CLOSE. IT IS ALSO THE ONLY THING ON THE MENU THAT HAS NEVER CHANGED. IT'S THE SIMPLEST THING TO MAKE IN THE ENTIRE BOOK. YOU BUY A FEW TASTY THINGS AND PUT THEM TOGETHER ON A TOOTHPICK OR SKEWER. THAT'S IT.

GILDAS

WHITE ANCHOVY, PICKLED PEPPER, AND MANZANILLA OLIVE

One of the most satisfying moments for a chef, a sommelier, or any home cook is to surprise a guest. Pleasantly, that is. One of the beautiful things about pintxos is that they are only a bite or two, and accordingly are a very low-risk way to try something new. So with that, we ask you to start your meal with an anchovy.

Too often, in my mind, I hear Gildas described as "mild white anchovies with pickled peppers and olives." The "mild" bothers me because a) white anchovies are inherently mild, and b) the terrific ones that we use (from Ortiz) are incredibly flavorful. But I understand the idea: folks need to be persuaded that our anchovies won't deliver the fishy punch associated with the common canned variety. Unlike "black anchovies" (see page 18), which are fully salt-cured, white anchovies, called *boquerones* in Spain, are quickly cured in salt, then marinated in vinegar and oil, which produces their unique flavor and texture (but does not make them as shelf-stable as cured anchovies are, so always refrigerate your boquerones). This same process makes them white, and milder; they are the same fish, just processed differently. So, if calling these "mild" anchovies helps tempt a guest into trying a Gilda, then I suppose it's for the greater good.

At this point, I imagine you may be wondering how the combination of anchovy, pickled pepper, and olive came to be called a "Gilda." Well, in 1946, Rita Hayworth was the hottest thing in Hollywood. Six thousand miles away in San Sebastian, at a bar called Casa Vallés, the owner began to combine anchovies, peppers, and olives on a skewer. The salty and spicy bite apparently reminded guests of the piquant—that is, sexy—personality of Hayworth's eponymous character in the new film *Gilda*.

There's some science behind the magic as well. The salt and the acid, plus the bit of spice, all hit you on the back sides of your tongue and get your appetite going. Your mouth literally begins to water. It's not unlike a briny raw oyster with a bit of vinegary mignonette. Famed French gastronome Jean Anthelme Brillat-Savarin is often quoted for his belief that any great meal should begin with a hundred oysters. Four or five Gildas do the trick for me.

There's really no wrong way to assemble these, but I like to be able to eat all the components in one bite. In Spain, the ingredients are much less expensive, and they make large Gildas with several anchovies, peppers, and olives. We use just one of each, making a compact bite.

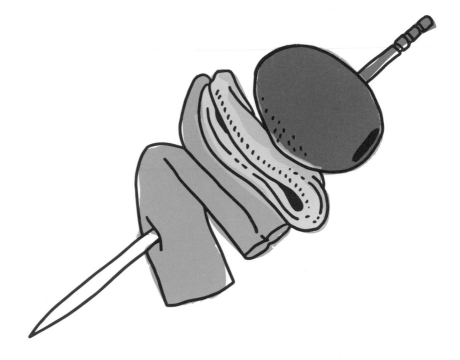

Begin by piercing an anchovy fillet, close to one end and centered, on a roughly 4-inch skewer or toothpick. Don't push the anchovy down towards the end of the stick—leave it ½ inch or so from the tip. Add an olive, wrap the anchovy over the olive, and skewer it again; this time you'll be skewering the (approximate) middle of the fillet. Now add a piece of pepper, then wrap the anchovy over that and skewer it one last time, near the opposite end of where you started. (Alternatively, if you'd like to keep it simpler, just skewer an olive, a folded anchovy, and a piece of pepper, as pictured above.) Repeat to assemble all of the pintxos.

The Gildas are best enjoyed immediately, but will keep in your fridge, tightly covered, for up to 3 days.

Makes 12 Gildas

12 boquerones (marinated white anchovy fillets) (we favor the Ortiz brand)

12 manzanilla or other briny green olives, pitted

4 pickled guindilla peppers (also known as piperra peppers), stems removed and cut crosswise into thirds

"BLACK GILDAS"

CURED ANCHOVY, PIQUILLO PEPPER, AND GARLIC CONFIT

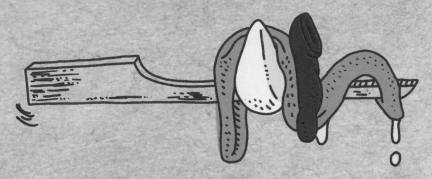

If white anchovies are the gateway anchovy (see recipe introduction, page 16), their cured, or "black," counterparts are for the established fans. These pack a stronger flavor—the salt they are cured in draws out moisture and intensifies the taste. The texture is also affected by the curing, and they may seem drier than white anchovies. But, if you enjoy that robust, fishy umami flavor, few things are better. There are just as many Gildas served in Spain with black anchovies as white.

Begin by piercing an anchovy fillet, close to one end and centered, on a roughly 4-inch skewer or toothpick. Don't push the anchovy down towards the end of the stick—leave it ½ inch or so from the tip. Add a strip of pepper, wrap the anchovy over the pepper, and skewer it again; this time you'll be skewering the (approximate) middle of the fillet. Now add a garlic clove, then wrap the anchovy over that and skewer it one last time, near the opposite end of where you started. Repeat to assemble all of the pintxos.

The Gildas are best enjoyed immediately, but will keep in your fridge, tightly covered, for up to 3 days.

NOTE: *To confit garlic, in a pot or small baking dish, cover peeled garlic cloves with olive oil and add a few sprigs of thyme and a bay leaf if you have them on hand. Place in a preheated 300°F oven for 90 minutes or until the garlic is tender and lightly browned. Let the garlic and oil cool and store, refrigerated, in an airtight container for up to a month. (A by-product of making the garlic confit is you now also have garlic oil, which you can use with mushrooms; see page 85).*

NOTE: *Piquillo is a sweet and meaty variety of pepper traditionally grown in Northern Spain. Its name is derived from "little beak," and they are the perfect size to stuff. It is almost always roasted, peeled, and then conserved in a jar or can, so all recipes in this book are for piquillos treated in this manner. They are now widely available, but if you are struggling to source them, roasted red bell peppers make an adequate substitute.*

Makes 12 Gildas

12   anchoas (cured black anchovy fillets) (we use the Don Bocarte brand)

4   canned or jarred piquillo peppers, cut crosswise into thirds

12   cloves Garlic Confit (see Note)

Sardinas y Rábanos

SARDINES AND RADISHES

Butter and radishes . . . sometimes that's all you need (well, salt, too). But add just a few more elements and you can elevate a simple snack into a beautiful pintxo. As with any simple, bare-bones dish, good ingredients are the key to success. We like to use Ortiz canned (or jarred) sardines, but there is a slew of terrific canned sardines available these days. Likewise, using beautiful radishes, good butter, and flaky, crunchy salt will make this bite sing.

Spread about 1 teaspoon butter on each toast. Place a sardine fillet, skin-side up, on each. Haphazardly shingle a few radish slices on top of each sardine. Finish the toasts with a couple drops each of lemon juice and olive oil, a few flakes of salt, and a parsley leaf.

NOTE: *If you are working with whole canned sardines, using a butter knife and your fingers, gently lift off the spine and then separate the fillets; use 6 whole fish to get the 12 fillets you need for this recipe.*

Makes 12 toasts

4   tablespoons unsalted butter, at room temperature (give it at least 30 minutes to soften)

12 slices baguette, lightly toasted

12 canned sardine fillets, packed in olive oil (see Note)

6   radishes (any variety), sliced into thin rounds

Juice of ¼ lemon

1   tablespoon olive oil

Sea salt (we love Maldon, a flaky sea salt from England)

12 leaves fresh flat-leaf parsley

ENSALADILLA RUSA CON ATÚN

RUSSIAN SALAD WITH TUNA

The Spanish dish known as "Russian Salad" is, simply put, potato salad with additional vegetables. It's known by this name throughout Latin America and much of Europe—and does indeed hail from Russia, where it's called "Olivier." I consider peas and carrots to be non-negotiable, but from there the possibilities are pretty much endless, including beets, fennel, onions, parsnips, pickles, even eggs and diced chicken or ham. And once the salad is piled on toasts, you have another world of choices for adding a top layer—in this case, top-notch canned tuna.

Put the potatoes in a small pot and cover with cold water. Add the bay leaf, thyme, black peppercorns, and a large pinch of salt and bring to a simmer over high heat. Lower the heat to maintain a bare simmer and cook the potatoes until tender when pierced with a knife, about 20 minutes. Drain the potatoes, discarding the bay leaf, thyme, and peppercorns.

While the potatoes are cooking, bring another small saucepan of water to a boil over high heat and add a large pinch of salt. Prepare an ice bath by filling a large bowl with equal parts ice and water. Add the carrots to the boiling water and cook until tender, about 4 minutes. Using a slotted spoon, transfer the carrots to the ice bath. Let the water return to boiling, add the peas, and blanch until tender; frozen peas only need about 30 seconds, while fresh will take 2 to 3 minutes. Using the slotted spoon, plunge the peas into the ice bath with the carrots. Let everything cool in the ice bath for about 5 minutes.

When the potatoes are cool enough to handle, break them into pieces that are just slightly larger than the peas and carrots. Drain the carrots and peas and pat dry.

Combine the potatoes, carrots, and peas in a large bowl. Drizzle the olive oil and lemon juice over the top and toss gently to coat. Add the mayonnaise, parsley, and fennel fronds, if using, and fold gently until well mixed. Taste and adjust the seasoning. The salad will keep, refrigerated in an airtight container, for up to 3 days. Bring to room temperature and taste before serving; adjust the seasoning with more salt and lemon juice as needed.

To assemble the toasts, arrange a heaping spoonful of the salad on each baguette slice and top each with a generous flake or two of the tuna. Garnish with sea salt and serve immediately.

Makes 12 pintxos

½   pound fingerling or other small waxy potatoes

1   bay leaf

2   sprigs fresh thyme

5   black peppercorns

    Salt, plus sea salt to garnish

2   medium carrots, peeled and cut into small dice (about pea-sized)

1   cup English peas, fresh or frozen

2   tablespoons olive oil

1   tablespoon fresh lemon juice, plus more as needed

1   cup good-quality mayonnaise

1   tablespoon chopped fresh flat-leaf parsley

1   tablespoon chopped fennel fronds (optional)

12   slices baguette, lightly toasted (optional)

6   ounces best-quality canned tuna (preferably Spanish and packed in olive oil), drained and flaked

ENSALADA DE HUEVOS Y CAMARONES

EGG SALAD AND SHRIMP TOASTS

These toasts remind me of my twenty-first birthday, which was spent at Los Gatos, a kitschy pintxo bar in Madrid. I honestly can't recall if this particular pintxo was served that night, but it's just the sort of thing I remember lining the glass-enclosed shelves atop their bar. These bites are super simple to assemble, and almost all of the work can be done ahead of time. The key is the generous splash of lemon juice we squeeze over these just before serving.

To make the poached shrimp, combine the water and salt in a saucepot and bring to a boil over high heat.

Meanwhile, prepare an ice bath by filling a large bowl with equal parts ice and water.

Remove the pot of boiling water from the heat and add the shrimp. Stir the shrimp around for about 90 seconds. Using a slotted spoon, transfer the shrimp to the ice bath. Let the shrimp cool completely (about 3 minutes), then drain and pat dry. Cut in half lengthwise and transfer to a bowl. Drizzle lightly with the olive oil and toss to coat. (If not using immediately, store in an airtight container in the fridge for up to 2 days.)

To make the egg salad, in a large bowl, combine the hard-boiled eggs, onion, celery, and parsley and toss gently to mix well. Add the mayo, lemon juice, and olive oil and stir to mix, then season with salt and black pepper (start with a pinch of salt and a few turns of your pepper mill).

To assemble the toasts, arrange a heaping spoonful of the egg salad on each baguette slice, then top each with a piece of shrimp. (If the shrimp has been refrigerated, let come to room temperature for a few minutes before using.) Squeeze a few drops of lemon juice over the shrimp and sprinkle just a hint of the chile powder over all. Serve immediately.

NOTE: *Our favorite trick for quickly and evenly chopping hard-boiled eggs is to push them through a wire rack—the kind usually used as a cooling rack or to line a baking sheet for roasting.*

Makes 12 toasts

For the poached shrimp:

- 4 cups water
- 3 tablespoons kosher salt
- 8 jumbo (21/25 count) shrimp, peeled (tails removed) and deveined (see page 148)
- 1 tablespoon olive oil

For the egg salad:

- 5 large eggs, hard-boiled, peeled, and cut into thumbnail-sized pieces (see Note)
- ¼ cup finely diced red onion
- ¼ cup finely diced celery
- 1 tablespoon chopped fresh flat-leaf parsley
- 2 tablespoons mayonnaise
- Juice of 1 lemon
- 1 teaspoon olive oil
- Salt and freshly ground black pepper

- 16 slices baguette, lightly toasted
- 1 lemon, cut into wedges, seeds removed
- 1 teaspoon Espellete or other chile powder

Plaza de Huertas

«BANDERILLA»

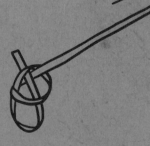

MIXED PICKLE SKEWERS

Say what you want about bullfighting, its impact on Spanish culture cannot be disputed—just ask Hemingway. Everything around the sport seems imbued with a special meaning, including the *banderilla*, the brightly decorated dart used to spear the bull before the final thrust of the sword. However, Northern Spaniards, in particular, tend to be against the controversial pastime; perhaps this is why they prefer their banderillas to be of the edible variety.

The category of pintxos named after this flamboyant weapon are skewers or toothpicks decorated with various pickled or marinated items. With so many grocers now offering a large selection of olives, pickles, and quality canned goods, there's little more to this pintxo than buying tasty stuff and skewering it. Any single component of this recipe is optional and can be omitted or replaced with another item.

If desired, the day before (or up to 1 week before) assembling the skewers, in a bowl, make the mojo, omitting the almonds. Add the Manchego cubes and stir to coat. Refrigerate overnight or for up to 1 week (or skip this step entirely if pressed for time).

To cook the quail eggs, bring a saucepan of water to a boil. Meanwhile, prepare an ice bath by filling a large bowl with equal parts ice and water and set aside. Reduce the heat under the boiling water to maintain a gentle simmer, add the quail eggs, and cook for 3½ minutes. Using a slotted spoon, transfer the eggs immediately to the ice bath. After they have cooled for about 1 minute, crack them slightly to allow water to run between the shells and egg whites for easier peeling. Let cool for about 5 minutes longer. Drain and peel carefully. (Note that you'll have 4 extra eggs, in case any aren't up to snuff.)

Using thin skewers or long toothpicks (thicker skewers may cause some of the items to split and fall off), assemble 16 banderillas, threading 1 cheese cube, 1 quail egg, 1 cornichon, 1 pickled onion, and 1 piquillo strip on each, in whatever order you please. Like Gildas, these are best enjoyed immediately or within a day or two, but can be refrigerated and stored for up to a few days.

Makes 16 skewers

1   batch Mojo Picón (page 84), almonds omitted (optional)

4   ounces young Manchego cheese (aged 3 months or less), cut into 16 cubes (about ½ inch), and marinated (optional)

20 quail eggs

16 cornichons

16 Pickled Pearl Onions (page 45)

4   piquillo peppers, each stemmed and cut lengthwise into 4 strips

Rollos de Pepino con Trucha

Trout Salad in Cucumber Rolls

When creating a lineup of a pintxos for your party (or for your restaurant), it is important to have at least one or two that require no work "on the pickup"—that is, when the dish is ordered—but rather have all the work done ahead of time. This is one of those—the only trick is slicing the cucumbers thinly enough that you can roll them, but not so thinly that the moisture of the trout salad causes the cucumbers to lose their pleasing crunch. We smoke the trout in house, but you can most certainly make this dish with store-bought smoked trout or, frankly, any other hot-smoked fish.

If you don't have a mandoline, consider getting one—but you can also make the super-thin cucumber slices needed here with a vegetable peeler or a sharp chef's knife, if you have good skills and work carefully.

Makes 16 skewers

2   6-ounce fillets smoked trout, homemade (page 39) or store-bought, bones removed, flaked into small chunks

¼   cup finely diced red onion

¼   cup finely diced celery

1   tablespoon minced fresh chives

⅔   cup mayonnaise

1   teaspoon olive oil, plus more for drizzling

1   lemon, halved

    Sea salt and freshly ground black pepper

2   medium (about 5-inch) Kirby cucumbers, scrubbed

In a large bowl, combine the trout, onion, celery, chives, mayonnaise, 1 teaspoon olive oil, and the juice of 1 lemon half. Stir to mix thoroughly. Season with salt and pepper. (The trout salad will keep, tighty covered in your fridge, for up to 3 days.)

Using a mandoline and working with one cuke at a time, slice the cucumbers very thinly lengthwise. (The first couple of slices will be too small to make rolls with, but use them to test the thickness. You want the slices to be as thick as possible while still being able to curl.) When you reach the seeds on one side, flip the cucumber and repeat the process on the other side. Depending on the size of the cucumber, you should be able to get at least 4 viable slices on each side before reaching the seeds.

Lay 16 cucumber slices out on a cutting board, plate, or tray. Sprinkle lightly with salt and let sit for 5 minutes. (This will draw out some moisture and make them more pliable.)

To assemble the rolls, place about 1 tablespoon of the trout salad ½ inch from the end of each cucumber slice. Lift the tail of the cucumber up and over the salad, tuck the end in to enclose it, and then keep rolling to create a tight cylinder. Repeat to assemble all the rolls.

To serve, gently arrange the rolls on a plate. Drizzle a bit of olive oil over the top, followed by a squeeze of lemon juice from the remaining lemon half, a sprinkle of sea salt, and a few grindings of pepper. Serve immediately, or cover and refrigerate for up to 3 hours. (They will last a little longer, but the cucumber will lose any crunch.)

PiQUILLOS RELLENOS

PEPPERS STUFFED WITH GOAT CHEESE AND CATALAN GREENS

Roasted piquillo peppers are one of the most common ingredients to find among the array of pintxos lining the bars in northern Spain. Their mild sweetness and meatiness make them perfect for stuffing. Salt cod and braised beef are traditional options, but this vegetarian version is inspired by the classic ravioli filling of ricotta and greens. Here goat cheese replaces the ricotta, and we added pine nuts and raisins to the greens—just as they do in Cataluña.

Pull the chard leaves off the stems and chop them roughly. Trim off the ends of the stems and dice. Set the leaves and stems aside separately.

Heat 2 tablespoons of the olive oil in a large sauté pan over medium heat. Add the onion, garlic, and chard stems and cook, stirring occasionally, until the onion is tender, about 10 minutes. Add the chopped chard leaves to the pan and stir until wilted, 1 or 2 minutes longer. Remove from the heat and allow the mixture to cool slightly. Season with salt and black pepper—go light on the salt, as the goat cheese that will be added is likely salty.

Preheat the oven to 375°F.

Transfer the chard mixture to a large bowl. Add the goat cheese, pine nuts, and raisins and stir to mix well. Scoop the filling into a pastry bag fitted with a ½-inch round tip or a large ziplock bag. If using a ziplock bag, cut off a corner to create a ½-inch hole. Using the bag, pipe the goat cheese mixture into the peppers to fill them, using about 3 tablespoons each.

Place an ovenproof sauté pan over high heat. Let the pan heat up for a good 2 minutes. Add the remaining 1 tablespoon olive oil, then arrange the stuffed peppers in the pan, making sure they are spaced as widely as possible. Sear for 3 minutes. (The natural sugars in the peppers will encourage them to caramelize deeply.) Using tongs, carefully flip the peppers. Transfer the pan of peppers to the oven and roast to sear the second side and to make sure the filling is nice and hot, about 5 minutes.

Remove the pan from the oven. Pour the vinegar into the pan and deglaze it, scraping up any browned bits on the bottom. Serve immediately, drizzled with the pan sauce.

Makes 12 stuffed peppers

1	bunch Swiss chard (spinach and kale work well, too)
3	tablespoons olive oil
1	medium yellow onion, diced
2	cloves garlic, thinly sliced
	Salt and freshly ground black pepper
8	ounces goat cheese
2	tablespoons pine nuts, toasted
2	tablespoons golden raisins, soaked in hot water for about 30 minutes, then drained
12	piquillo peppers, stemmed and seeded
2	tablespoons sherry vinegar

CROQUETAS DE GARBANZOS

CHICKPEA CROQUETTES WITH OLIVE AÏOLI

We love traditional Spanish béchamel-based croquettes (see page 28), but they require a good deal of work! They also contain everything that so many folks want to avoid these days: gluten, dairy, meat—not to mention plenty of fat. Our chickpea croquettes, essentially the *panisse* served in nearby southern France, avoid all those categories (at least until you dip them in aïoli). They are quite tasty, none-theless, and have the added benefit of taking a fraction of the time to prepare.

We like to serve *croquetas de garbanzos* with our Olive Aïoli. You could also buy tapenade and simply whisk that into your mayonnaise.

In a 4-quart saucepan, combine the olive oil and garlic over medium-low heat. Allow the garlic to toast, stirring often, but once it shows the first sign of browning, add the water and salt.

Raise the heat to medium-high and bring the water to a boil, then reduce the heat to maintain a bare simmer. Add the chickpea flour, whisking feverishly. Once the mixture has come together, reduce the heat to low. Cook the croqueta batter, whisking every minute or so, until a uniformly dense texture is achieved, about 5 minutes. Stir in the chives.

Line a small (8-by-10-inch) baking sheet with parchment paper. Scoop the batter onto the prepared pan, spreading it evenly and pushing it into the corners. Place in the refrigerator, uncovered, and let cool completely, about 1 hour. (At this point, you can cover the batter tightly and store it in the fridge for up to 4 days.) Once cooled, turn the batter out onto a cutting board and cut it into squares. Any size will work, but we find that a 1½-inch square makes for a nice two-biter.

While the batter is cooling, make the Olive Aïoli: In a blender or food processor, combine the Aïoli and olives and process until chunky or smooth, as you like.

When you are ready to serve, pour canola oil into a deep fryer or 4-quart pot to a depth of at least 4 inches and heat over medium-high heat to 375°F. Using a slotted spoon or skimmer, carefully add a handful of croquettes to the hot oil, being sure not to crowd the pan, and fry until golden brown, about 3 minutes. Transfer to a plate lined with paper towels to drain, and sprinkle with salt while still hot. Repeat to fry the remaining croquetas.

Serve hot, with the aïoli.

Makes about thirty-two 1½-inch square *croquetas*

2	tablespoons olive oil
3	cloves garlic, grated on a Microplane
4	cups water
2	tablespoons kosher salt, plus for more finishing
2¼	cups chickpea flour, sifted
3	tablespoons minced chives or any chopped "soft" herb, such as parsley, cilantro, or dill

For the Olive Aïoli:

2	cups Aïoli (see page 80)
1	cup meaty black olives, such as Empeltre or Kalamata, pitted

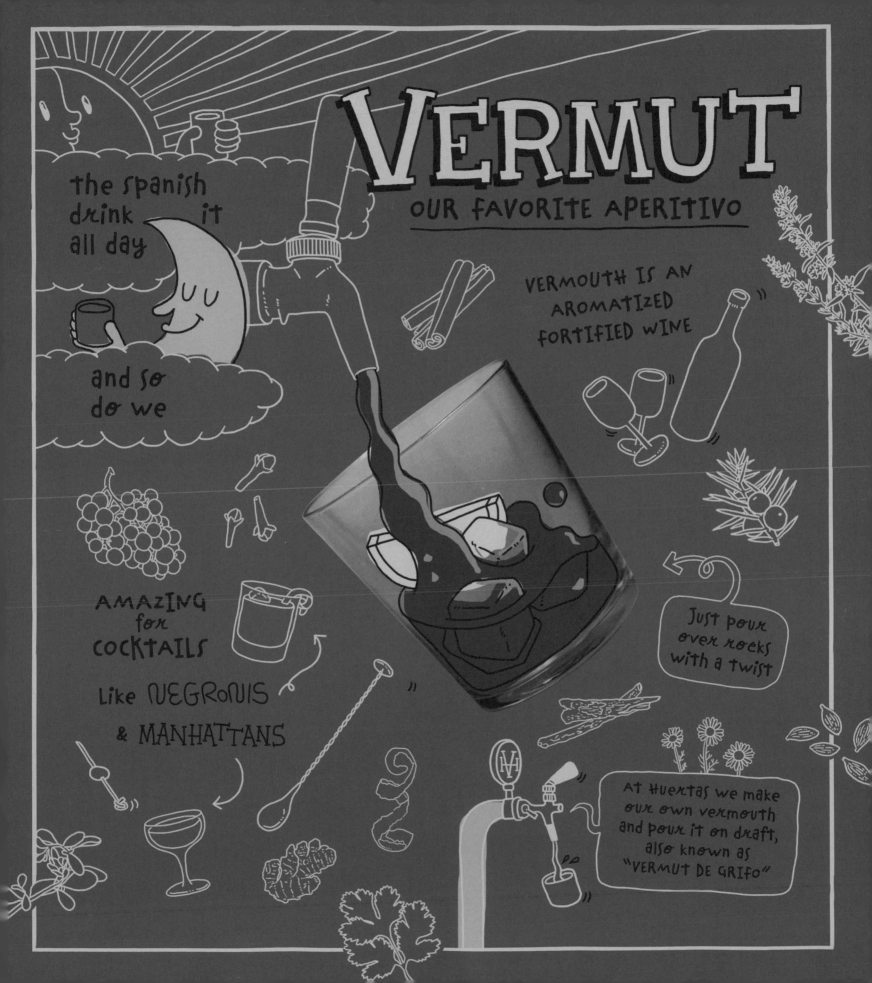

CROQUETAS DE PATO

DUCK CROQUETTES

A true crowd-pleaser! Béchamel-based croquettes are a staple throughout Spain, but I was reluctant to put them on our menu. I viewed them as, well, junk food—the macaroni and cheese of pintxos, something that is satisfying because of fattiness rather than flavor. But then we put duck breast on the menu, so we needed to find a use for the accompanying legs, fat, and bones. We ended up developing a recipe that elevated *croquetas*, the "chicken fingers of Spain," to a different level. This sophisticated version replaces some of the butter with duck fat, and some of the milk with duck stock, and the legs, made into confit, are folded into the mix.

Note the trick to breading these croquettes is in the final step: Because the balls are gooey and nearly liquid inside after they're fried in the hot oil, it's crucial to create a strong crust. Accordingly, instead of a typical three-step breading process that uses flour plus eggs plus crumbs, we bread them with crumbs, then eggs, then more crumbs.

In a saucepan over medium-low heat, warm the duck stock and milk together. Bring to a bare simmer. While the milk and stock heat, pull the duck confit meat off the bones, transfer to a food processor, and pulse until finely shredded. You should have about 1½ cups. Set aside.

Meanwhile, in a large skillet, melt the butter and duck fat. Add the onion and garlic and let them sweat, stirring occasionally. When they are starting to soften but have not yet taken on color, add the thyme and season with salt and pepper. Add the flour and cook for about 1 minute, stirring constantly.

Add the warm stock mixture to the skillet. Bring to a simmer, whisking constantly, until the batter starts to thicken. Add the reserved duck confit meat and cook, stirring, until the duck meat is warm and evenly dispersed—about 2 more minutes. Taste and adjust the seasoning. Pour into a heatproof tray or dish and let cool. (At this point the croquette mixture will keep, covered in the refrigerator, for up to 3 days. Don't cover until the mixture is cool, otherwise the steam and condensation will affect the texture.)

Once cooled, scoop up large pinches of the croquette mixture and roll between your palms into balls about 1 inch in diameter. It helps to either wet your hands with water or grease them with a bit of olive oil so the mixture doesn't stick. (An even easier way to get uniform croquettes is to use a small ice-cream scoop.) Place the balls on a baking sheet as you work. When all of the mixture is rolled, transfer the tray to the fridge for about 30 minutes (or the freezer for about 10 minutes) to help set the shape.

Makes about thirty-five 1-inch square *croquetas*

1½	cups duck stock (you can sub chicken stock)
1½	cups milk
2	confited duck legs, finely shredded
2	tablespoons unsalted butter
1	tablespoon plus 2 teaspoons duck fat
1	medium Spanish onion, finely diced
2	cloves garlic, finely diced
2	teaspoons chopped fresh thyme
	Salt and freshly ground black pepper
¾	cup all-purpose flour
3	cups plain dried bread crumbs
3	large eggs
	Canola oil for frying

Meanwhile, set up two large, shallow bowls. Pour the bread crumbs into one and beat the eggs in the other. Working with about 5 croquettes at a time, toss them first in the bread crumbs to coat thoroughly, then transfer to the beaten eggs and turn to coat thoroughly. Using a fork or slotted spoon, transfer them back to the bread crumbs. Roll them around gently to cover completely in a second layer of crumbs, then place on a clean baking sheet. Repeat until all the croquettes are coated. (At this point, they will keep, tightly covered in your fridge, for up to 3 days; or freeze carefully, without them sticking together, for up to 3 months.)

When you are ready to serve, pour canola oil to a depth of at least 4 inches into a deep fryer or 4-quart pot and heat over medium-high heat to 375°F. Using a slotted spoon or skimmer, carefully add a handful of croquettes to the hot oil, being sure not to crowd the pot, and fry until golden brown, about 3 minutes. Transfer to a plate lined with paper towels to drain, and season with salt while still hot. Repeat to fry the remaining croquetas.

Serve hot. No sauce necessary—you'll see!

VARIATIONS

To make different types of croquetas, simply replace the duck fat with butter and the duck stock and duck meat with a combination of your choosing, such as:

- Chicken stock and ground jamón

- Chicken stock and shredded chicken (and maybe add some minced jalapeños!)

- Shrimp stock or fish stock and minced shrimp

- Fish stock and flaked salt cod

- Mushroom Stock (page 115) and sautéed mushrooms

MANCHEGO CON MEMBRILLO

MANCHEGO AND QUINCE PASTE TOASTS

Manchego is the undisputed king of Spanish cheeses. Much like Parmesan, this means that there are countless inferior versions, but for this simple pintxo, a high-quality cheese makes all the difference. Look for raw (unpasteurized) Manchego; and the longer the cheese has been aged, the firmer, flakier, saltier, and more intense it will be. Besides bread, the only other ingredient here is *membrillo*, Spain's famous quince paste. This is now widely available in specialty-foods and online stores, but below is the recipe for ours. Traditionally, the paste is cooked to a firmness that can be sliced; we like to leave it a bit looser so that it can easily be used as a spread.

To make the membrillo, peel the lemon and set the peels aside. Cut the lemon in half. Fill a large bowl halfway with water and squeeze in the juice of one lemon half.

Peel the quince, transferring each to the lemon water to prevent oxidation as you work. Once peeled, remove the quince from the lemon water one by one; cutting around the core, cut them into large (about 2-inch) chunks. Return the chunks to the bowl of water as you work. Discard the cores.

Makes 16 toasts

For the membrillo:

1	lemon
2	pounds quince (about 4 fruits)
⅓	cup water
½	vanilla bean, split, or ⅓ teaspoon vanilla extract
2	cups sugar
16	slices baguette, lightly toasted
4	ounces Manchego cheese

Combine the quince, lemon peel, and water in a heavy-bottomed pot (see Note). Scrape the seeds from the vanilla bean into the pot and drop in the pod. Cover and cook over low heat for about 1 hour. Every 10 minutes or so, give the quince a stir and make sure nothing is sticking to the bottom; if it is, add a little more water.

Once the quince is tender (stick a fork into a piece; there should be no resistance), pour the contents of the pot into a strainer or colander placed in the sink. Discard the strained liquid and vanilla bean and transfer the cooked quince and lemon peel to a blender with the juice of the remaining lemon half. Blend on high speed to create a smooth purée.

Pour the purée into a heavy-bottomed saucepan and stir in the sugar. Cover with a lid or splatter screen and cook over very, very low heat (the sugar makes it easy to scorch the bottom of the pan), stirring occasionally and making sure to scrape the bottom. Cook for 30 to 45 minutes, until the color has darkened to a deep amber. Remove from the heat and let cool, uncovered. The paste will keep, in an airtight container in the fridge, for up to 2 months.

To assemble the pintxo, spread a layer of membrillo over the bread. Depending on the age and texture of the Manchego, slice it, break it into chunks, or crumble it by hand. Place some cheese over the membrillo on each toast and serve.

NOTE: *If you have a pressure cooker, this is a great time to use it. We combine the quince, lemon peel, vanilla bean and seeds, and water in a pressure cooker and cook on high for 20 minutes.*

CONSERVAS

IN SPAIN, canned seafood is a delicacy, not something kids dread finding in their lunch boxes. The Iberian Peninsula has the Atlantic Ocean and Mediterranean Sea covering all but a small portion of its borders, and inland, the four saltwater inlets called the Rías Baixas run through Galicia, adding up to a vast array of seafood products locally available. Vigo, in Galicia, is the second-largest fishing port in the world (behind only Tokyo). Much of Spain's seafood, even the top-quality stuff, goes into a can. Spaniards recognize that and will pay a premium to simply have a bartender pass them a can of mussels, scallops, or octopus and a toothpick.

Even without any special equipment, it's easy to preserve fish and other foods at home with techniques like smoking and pickling—perhaps not to last for years, but weeks or months at least, and all the while developing unique and pleasing flavors and textures. The recipes in this chapter not only increase shelf life, they offer new, interesting, and delicious ways for home cooks to enhance fish, meat, and vegetables.

MUSSELS

WHY NOT SOME LEMON?

WHITE ANCHOVIES

CONTROL DE CALIDAD 18

BLACK ANCHOVIES

MACKEREL

TUNA

SCALLOPS

SQUID

SARDINES

CLAMS

MEJILLONES EN ESCABECHE

MARINATED MUSSELS

Of all the Spanish *conservas*, mussels in escabeche, sometimes called marinated or pickled mussels, have gained the most popularity outside of Spanish kitchens. In New York alone, dozens of restaurant serve mussels treated in this way. It's not surprising, given that they are delicious, simple, and inexpensive. They are great straight up, on toast with aïoli, or skewered as part of a Banderilla (see page 23).

In a large, heavy-bottomed pot with a tight-fitting lid, heat 2 tablespoons of the olive oil over medium heat. Add 2 of the garlic cloves and toast for 1 minute. Add the wine and mussels, cover tightly, and steam for 3 minutes. Lift the lid every 30 seconds or so to see if the mussels have opened; depending on the mussels, they could all open in 3 minutes, or it may take up to an additional 5 minutes.

When all (or nearly all) the mussels have opened, remove them from the heat and dump the contents of the pot into a colander placed over a bowl to catch the broth. Discard any mussels that failed to open. Set the mussels aside to cool. Pour the broth through a fine-mesh strainer (lined with cheesecloth, if you have it) to remove any sand or grit. Set the mussel broth aside.

Make the escabeche: While the mussels are cooling, in a small saucepan, combine the ¼ cup remaining olive oil and the remaining 2 cloves garlic. Turn the burner to medium and toast the garlic, turning once or twice, until lightly browned, about 3 minutes. Remove from the heat and add the pimentón and bay leaf. After the pimentón blooms for a minute, add the vinegar and whisk to combine.

When the mussels are cool, shuck them and combine them with the escabeche in a bowl and toss together. Transfer the contents of the bowl to a small serving bowl or storage container and pour in the reserved mussel broth. The mussels should be completely covered in liquid; if not, add more oil and vinegar as needed (using a 1:2 ratio of oil to vinegar). The mussels will be great within a few hours, but can be refrigerated, tightly covered, for up to 1 week. They will be best, though, for about the first 2 days; after that, the vinegar may cause the mussels to toughen.

Makes 2 cups conserved mussels

- **2** tablespoons plus ¼ cup olive oil
- **4** cloves garlic, lightly crushed
- **½** cup dry white wine
- **1** pound bouchot mussels (or other plump variety of mussel), scrubbed and debearded
- **1** tablespoon sweet pimentón
- **2** fresh bay leaves, or 1 dried
- **½** cup Moscatel vinegar or other mild white wine vinegar

ALMEJAS EN ACEITE

CLAMS IN OIL

Holding a product in fat or oil is one of the simplest techniques for preserving. In this treatment of *almejas*, we steam the clams in a traditional manner, but instead of eating them immediately after shucking, we hold them in olive oil. Refrigerated, they keep for about a week (and if you happened to have the tools to pressure-can them, they would last indefinitely). You can easily vary the flavors by adding different or additional aromatics to the clams as they steam, or to the oil that you conserve the clams in.

We serve the clams with some toast, sea salt, a lemon wedge, and a salad or herbs and shaved fennel. A little butter or aïoli on the toast is nice, too.

TO PURGE THE CLAMS, ADD THEM AND A HANDFUL OF SALT TO A BOWL, PLACE IN THE SINK, AND RUN UNDER COLD WATER FOR 5 TO 10 MINUTES, SHAKING THE CLAMS VIGOROUSLY A FEW TIMES.

Makes 2 cups conserved clams

- 2 tablespoons plus 2 cups olive oil
- 5 cloves garlic, lightly crushed
- 1 teaspoon red pepper flakes
- 1 handful fresh flat-leaf parsley stems or fennel fronds (or both)
- 2 pounds clams (any clam will work, but smaller varieties tend to be more tender; we usually use cockles), scrubbed and purged (see Note above)
- ½ cup dry white wine
- 1 teaspoon fennel seeds
- 1 teaspoon black peppercorns
- 1 lemon

In a large, heavy-bottomed pot with a tight-fitting lid, heat 2 tablespoons of the olive oil over medium heat. Add 4 of the garlic cloves and toast for 1 minute. Add the red pepper flakes and parsley and toast for 15 seconds, then add the clams, discarding any open shellfish that do not close to the touch. Add the wine. Cover tightly and steam for 3 minutes. Lift the lid every 30 seconds or so to see if they have opened; depending on the type of clams, they could all open in 3 minutes, or it may take up to an additional 5 minutes.

When all (or nearly all) the clams have opened, remove them from the heat and dump the contents of the pot into a colander placed over a bowl to catch the broth. Discard any clams that failed to open and set the clams aside to cool. Pour the broth through a fine-mesh strainer (lined with cheesecloth, if you have it) into another container to remove any sand or grit. Refrigerate the clam broth for another use for up to 4 days or freeze indefinitely.

While the clams are cooling, in a small saucepan, toast the fennel seeds and peppercorns over medium heat until fragrant, 2 to 3 minutes. Using a vegetable peeler, remove the lemon skin in 5 or 6 finger-sized pieces. Pour the remaining 2 cups olive oil into a serving bowl or storage container and add the toasted spices, along with the lemon peel.

When the clams are cool, shuck them and add to the seasoned oil. Cover tightly and refrigerate for at least 4 hours and up to 5 days. Before serving, allow the clams and oil to come to room temperature until the oil is no longer congealed, about 20 minutes.

TRUCHA AHUMADA

SMOKED TROUT

One of the original means of preserving fish or meat was to smoke it. We continue to smoke food with great regularity, but typically the purpose is to add flavor rather than extend shelf life. Eating in Spain, I'm always surprised how many cured and smoked fish items you see—some of my favorite foods that I associate with my hometown's Jewish-deli culture.

The technique in this recipe is quite simple, but requires you to have some form of smoker. While smoking fish (or meat) indoors is not advisable, if your home is well ventilated or you have a strong kitchen hood, you can throw caution to the wind and create an indoor smoker (see below). Otherwise, use your outdoor grill or smoker.

The smoked trout is great in salads (page 83) or can be made into a salad itself (page 24).

Season the flesh side of the trout fillets with salt. Let the salt lightly cure the fish for 1 hour.

While the fish is curing, set up your smoker. Build a medium-hot fire in a charcoal grill or preheat a gas grill to medium. Depending on how much control you have over the temperature, you're looking for something between 250°F and 300°F. Time your smoke for when the fish is done curing.

Drain the wood chips, push the hot coals to a corner, and arrange the chips on top of the hot coals, or add to the smoker box of your gas grill. Arrange the fish on the grill rack, on the opposite side as the hot coals, to avoid direct heat, and cook until the fish flakes easily when nudged with a fork, 8 to 10 minutes.

Transfer the fish to a platter and let cool briefly, then serve. The smoked trout will keep, covered tightly in the refrigerator, for up to 2 weeks.

Makes 12 ounces smoked fish

2 6-ounce trout fillets, bones removed

Kosher salt

1 cup apple wood chips, soaked in water for at least 30 minutes

SMOKING INDOORS

PLACE two layers of aluminum foil over the bottom of a wide shallow heavy-bottomed pan with a tight-fitting lid. Next, place a handful of soaked and drained wood chips on the foil and spread them out evenly. Position a rack or steamer basket above the chips. There needs to be a few inches of space between the rack and the lid, as this is where the fish will go.

COVER the pan tightly and place over medium heat. After about 5 minutes, open the lid slightly to peek, and see if smoke pours out; if not, re-cover and wait a couple more minutes. Keep checking every 2 minutes until the smoke builds nicely. Once the smoke is thick, working quickly, remove the lid, place the seasoned fish fillets (see above) on the rack, and cover the pot again. Smoke until the fillets flake easily when nudged with a fork, 8 to 12 minutes.

CABALLA EN VINAGRE

PICKLED MACKEREL

This simple technique for pickling fish and then holding them in olive oil works beautifully for any number of small fish, such as sardines or anchovies.

Unlike other methods of conserving, such as escabeche, *en vinagre* fish is never cooked with heat, but rather is cured by packing it in salt and then pickling it in vinegar, where it "cooks" in much the same way as fish is tenderized by the citrus juice in ceviche.

Cut each fillet in half lengthwise, on either side of the pin bones (the small bones running down the middle of each fillet). Discard the pin bones and attached flesh.

Line a nonreactive dish (glass is good) just large enough to hold all of the mackerel pieces (and with sides at least 1 inch tall) with about one-third of the salt. Place the mackerel pieces, skin-side down, on the salt, then cover completely with the remaining salt. Let cure for 1 hour.

Remove the mackerel from the salt and rinse the fish and the dish well. Return the mackerel to the clean dish and pour over the vinegar. Let the mackerel pickle at room temperature for 1 hour.

In a serving bowl or a storage container, combine the olive oil, thyme, and garlic. Transfer the pickled mackerel to the seasoned oil. The mackerel is immediately ready to eat and will keep, tightly covered in the refrigerator, for up to 2 weeks. Before serving, allow the fish and oil to come to room temperature, about 20 minutes or until the oil is no longer congealed. The pickled mackerel is great as part of a salad, on toast, or sliced and added to a Banderilla (page 23).

Makes 12 ounces pickled fish

2	mackerel fillets, about 6 ounces each
4	cups kosher salt
2	cups Chardonnay vinegar or other mild white vinegar
2	cups olive oil
5	sprigs fresh thyme
2	cloves garlic, lightly crushed

CONFIT DE ATÚN

TUNA CONFIT

While the south of France—Nice in particular—is famous for oil-poached tuna, Spain is where most of it comes from. Fishermen off the southern coast of Spain use a sophisticated setup of nets strung across the Strait of Gibraltar to capture what many consider to be the best tuna in the world. The highest-quality canned tunas can be terribly expensive, so not only is it simple and more rewarding to make your own tender, rich tuna confit, it is often more economical.

In a bowl, stir together the salt, peppercorns, fennel seeds, thyme, and lemon zest. Rub the tuna pieces on all sides with the seasoning and let sit at room temperature, lightly curing, for 45 minutes.

While the fish is curing, make the confit oil: Combine all the ingredients in a large pot and place over medium-low heat; you want to warm the oil gently to allow the herbs and spices to infuse it. Heat the oil until it registers between 170°F and 180°F on a candy, deep-frying, or instant-read thermometer. Turn the heat as low as possible while still maintaining temperature. If it gets too hot, turn your burner off for a few seconds (or a few minutes).

After the tuna has cured for 45 minutes, rinse it and pat dry with paper towels. Check one more time that the oil is in the proper temperature range, then, using a slotted spoon or a skimmer, carefully lower the tuna into the warm seasoned oil and poach for 10 to 12 minutes, depending on how pink you want the center.

Using the slotted spoon or skimmer, transfer the oil-poached tuna to a serving plate or individual plates. You can serve it warm immediately (seasoned with a few drops of lemon juice and a sprinkle of salt if necessary), but we usually let it cool slightly, then flake it into a few large chunks and hold it in the confit oil until serving.

To store, let the seasoned oil cool to room temperature. Transfer the tuna to an airtight container (or containers) and pour in the oil to cover. Store, tightly covered in the refrigerator, for up to 2 weeks. (Note that the tuna confit will only hold this long if it is completely submerged in the oil.)

Makes 1 pound confited tuna

- 1 cup coarse sea salt, such as La Baleine
- 1 teaspoon cracked black peppercorns
- 1 teaspoon toasted fennel seeds
- ½ teaspoon minced fresh thyme
- Zest of 1 lemon
- 1 pound tuna, cut into planks roughly 2 inches wide and 1 inch high

For the confit oil:

- 4 cups olive oil
- 8 cloves garlic
- 1 tablespoon black peppercorns
- 2 bay leaves
- 10 sprigs fresh thyme
- Zest of 1 lemon

ZANAHORIAS EN ESCABECHE

MARINATED CARROTS

Escabeche translates to "marinate," "brine," or simply "pickle," but, as in life, details get lost in translation—the Spanish approach is unique. Whereas most pickles we are accustomed to are raw vegetables that have been submerged in brine or fermented with salt, the Spanish way is to cook the item before pickling. In this way it ends up being something of what you could call a reverse marinade. This gives escabeche technique the added benefit that it can be used to preserve proteins—quail is traditional—that cannot be preserved simply by brining.

We fry the carrots for our escabeche to produce an even browning, but you can roast (or even grill) them instead. Note that this is a carrot dish, not just a dish with carrots—so it's worth it to seek out the tastiest, most beautiful ones you can find. These are great in salads, or served with cured meats or pâté, but we typically use them on toasts with whipped goat cheese and herbs.

Makes 4 cups

- **1** pound small (finger-sized) carrots, scrubbed but not peeled
- Canola oil for frying
- Salt and freshly ground black pepper
- **2** cups sherry vinegar or any other wine-based vinegar
- **⅔** cup olive oil
- **3** cloves garlic, lightly crushed
- **8** sprigs fresh thyme
- **2** bay leaves

If you can't find small carrots, use larger ones and cut them into similarly sized but somewhat irregular batons, about 4 inches long and ½ inch wide.

Pour canola oil into a deep fryer or 4-quart pot to a depth of 4 inches and heat to 375°F. Working in small batches so you do not crowd the pan, use a slotted spoon or skimmer to carefully add the carrots to the hot oil. Fry until they are dark brown—nearly burnt—and just tender enough to stick a fork through, about 5 minutes. Transfer to a plate lined with paper towels to drain, and season liberally (keeping in mind that some seasoning will fall off in the marinade) with salt and pepper while still hot.

(Alternatively, toss the carrots in a roasting pan with some olive oil, salt, and pepper, spread out in an even layer, and roast at 425°F for about 20 minutes, or until dark and tender as described.)

When the carrots are still very hot, toss them in a bowl with the vinegar, olive oil, garlic, thyme, and bay leaves. Cover the bowl tightly with plastic wrap to let the carrots steam and absorb the marinade. After about 30 minutes, transfer the carrots and marinade to an airtight container and refrigerate. Bring them back to room temperature before serving.

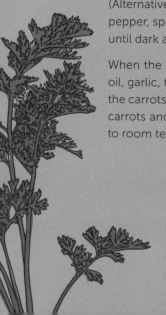

CEBOLLITAS EN VINAGRE

PICKLED PEARL ONIONS

When in doubt: pickles. When building a dish, texture and acid are two elements that should always be considered, and being able to add both at once is a great tool. Pickles are often a garnish, a complementary element, or a finishing touch—like how these tiny onions add flavor and a pleasing visual element to the sauce for the Pato a la Sevillana (page 124)—but when dressed up a bit and in creative combinations, they can become the star, as in the Banderilla *pintxo* (page 23).

The pickling brine below can be used for a multitude of vegetables, and depending on what you're pickling and whether you want a raw crunch or a more tender result, you can use the brine hot, cold, or at room temperature. You can also change the type of vinegar and use additional spices (consider fennel seeds, coriander, mustard seeds, etc.).

Put the onions in a small saucepan and add cold water to cover. Bring to a boil, then drain the onions. This will remove some of the assertiveness from the onions and begin to tenderize them.

Meanwhile, in a small pot, combine the 1⅓ cups water, the vinegar, sugar, salt, peppercorns, thyme, and bay leaf and bring to a simmer. Add the blanched onions; the onions will float, so you will need to weigh them down with a heatproof plate or a lid that is smaller than the pot. Simmer until tender, about 10 minutes. Remove from the heat and let cool to room temperature before using or storing. Refrigerated in an airtight container, the onions will keep in their brine for up to 3 months.

Makes about 1 quart

2	cups pearl onions, peeled
1⅓	cups water
2	cups white wine vinegar
⅔	cup sugar
1	teaspoon salt
1	teaspoon black peppercorns
4	sprigs fresh thyme
1	bay leaf

VARIATION: PICKLED RED ONIONS

Replace the pearl onions with 1 large red onion, thinly sliced. Skip the blanching step. In a pot, combine all the brine ingredients, substituting red wine vinegar for the white wine vinegar. Simmer and stir until the salt and sugar dissolve. Cool the brine to room temperature and then add the sliced onions. Refrigerate overnight. The onions can be used the next day and will maintain a pleasant crunch for up to a week.

Setas En Vinagre y Aceite

MARINATED MUSHROOMS

Briefly cooking mushrooms in a simmering pickle brine and then holding them in oil isn't a technique I picked up in Spain or read about in a book, but rather one of the many methods I learned in the years I spent working in great restaurants before opening my own. This recipe combines a number of techniques from this chapter. These mushrooms can be the star of a pintxo, but we usually use them as a complementary ingredient or finishing touch, as in the Arroz con Champiñones (page 109). They are terrific in salads, as well.

Trim the stem ends of the mushrooms. Using your hands, break the caps and stems into small pieces about the size of your thumb.

In a small saucepan, combine the vinegar, water, sugar, salt, 2 of the garlic cloves, 2 of the thyme sprigs, and 1 teaspoon of the peppercorns. Bring to a boil, stirring to help dissolve the sugar and salt. Reduce the heat to maintain a simmer and add half of the mushrooms. Cook for 1 minute. Using a spider or slotted spoon, transfer the mushrooms to a bowl. Repeat to cook the remaining mushrooms. (If you like, cool the pickling liquid, cover, and keep in the fridge to make another batch of mushrooms or another type of pickle. The liquid will hold indefinitely.)

Add the olive oil, bay leaves, and remaining 1 teaspoon peppercorns, 2 thyme sprigs, and 2 garlic cloves to the bowl with the mushrooms and toss to coat and distribute everything evenly. Pack tightly into an airtight container or containers; the mushrooms should be completely submerged. If not, add a bit more olive oil as needed.

Store in the fridge, tightly covered, for up to 3 weeks. Before serving, allow to come to room temperature until the oil is no longer congealed, about 20 minutes. They are great on toast with a bit of butter, aïoli, or goat cheese, or can be folded into a salad.

Makes 2 cups

8	ounces hen of the woods mushrooms (other mushrooms that work well are beech and pioppini)
2	cups sherry vinegar (or vinegar of your choosing; rice wine also works nicely)
1	cup water
½	cup sugar
1	teaspoon kosher salt
4	cloves garlic, lightly crushed
4	sprigs fresh thyme
2	teaspoons black peppercorns
1	cup olive oil
2	fresh bay leaves, or 1 dried

HuEvoS

WE CAN'T THINK of another cuisine in the world as dependent on eggs as Spanish. Inexpensive and protein-rich, eggs have long been essential to a country that struggled economically for much of the twentieth century. As a result, an array of egg-based dishes is central to Spain's regional traditions. Foremost among them is *tortilla española,* a rich potato-and-egg omelet resembling an Italian frittata. Infinite variations exist and others are always being improvised.

The same is true of two other egg mainstays on the Spanish table: *revueltos* (scrambled eggs) and egg dishes built around crispy *migas* (bread crumbs). One Spanish egg speciality that seldom veers from the classic version, *huevos rotos,* has become a mainstay on our menu, though we've found a number of ways to tweak the classic.

Beyond the diversity, what's unique is Spaniards' eagerness to eat *huevos* at any time of day or night. We have included several of our favorite iterations—and urge you not to be afraid of serving eggs for dinner!

TORTILLA ESPAÑOLA

SPANISH POTATO OMELET

It's difficult to find a restaurant or bar in Spain that doesn't serve *tortilla.* This dish—which, somewhat confusingly to the uninitiated, shares a name with the corn or flour rounds that elsewhere in the world are piled high with fillings—represents Spanish restaurant cuisine in many ways. For one, there is no shortage of potatoes or eggs in even the humblest corners of the country. Secondly, restaurant kitchens in Spain, particularly in the casual tapas bars that dominate the dining scene, are quite small, making it necessary to have as much as possible prepped ahead of time—items, that is, that can be served (often at room temperature) from directly behind the bar. This is usually the case with tortilla, meaning it's necessary to cook the eggs completely so that the tortilla can sit on the bar for hours until a bartender cuts off a wedge upon request.

However, most places that are known for their tortillas cook the omelet to order, usually leaving it a bit runny—just as we do. Historically in Spain, ovens are not necessarily common in either homes or restaurants, so our tortilla is cooked on top of the stove, which requires a good bit of finesse.

The following recipe represents our technique for making the classic Spanish tortilla, which departs from tradition by finishing the omelet in an oven under a broiler. We also added a couple of variations—one that substitutes a different root vegetable for the potatoes and one that shows how to add another layer of flavor to the mix. Let these inspire you; the potential variations are, of course, endless.

Preheat the oven to 350°F.

Heat 1 tablespoon of the olive oil in a sauté pan over medium heat. Add the onion and stir to coat in the oil. Cook until the onion begins to color, stirring occasionally to prevent burning or sticking, then reduce the heat to low and continue to cook very slowly, stirring often, until caramelized to a rich, deep golden brown, about 30 minutes total. If you find that the onion is sticking at any point, sprinkle in a tablespoon or so of water, and use your spoon to scrape up any browned bits that are stuck to the pan bottom. When you have achieved the desired color, add ½ teaspoon of the salt. (Adding the salt any earlier will draw water out of the onion and prevent it from caramelizing nicely.) Remove from the heat and let cool.

While the onion is caramelizing, pile the potato slices in a roasting pan. Drizzle with 4 tablespoons of the olive oil, season with 1 teaspoon of the salt, and toss to coat well. Roast until tender, about 15 minutes. You should be able to bend a potato slice without resistance, but it shouldn't break unless completely bent in half. Remove from the oven and set aside. Position an oven rack about 6 inches from the broiler and preheat the broiler on a low setting.

In a bowl, whisk together the eggs, cream, and thyme. Add the caramelized onions, roasted potatoes, and the remaining ½ teaspoon salt and fold gently to mix.

Heat a 6-inch ovenproof nonstick frying pan over medium heat for 1 to 2 minutes, then add 2 teaspoons of the remaining olive oil. If the pan is hot enough, the oil should dance, skidding around the pan rather than pooling. Pour in the potato and egg mixture and stir, as if making scrambled eggs, for 30 seconds, then turn the heat down to medium-low and stop stirring, allowing the eggs to settle on the bottom. Cook for 2 minutes, then transfer the pan to the rack set below the preheated broiler. Cook until the top is set but has just barely begun to brown, about 2 minutes longer. If you press down on the tortilla with a spoon or spatula, some runny eggs should ooze from the center. Remove from the oven.

Let the tortilla cool briefly, then tap the bottom of the pan firmly on your countertop a few times and transfer the tortilla to a plate by placing the plate upside-down on top of the pan, holding the bottom of the plate and the pan handle, and then quickly and carefully inverting the tortilla so it releases onto the plate.

Drizzle with the remaining 1 teaspoon olive oil. Cut into wedges and serve immediately.

Serves 3 as a breakfast or brunch entrée, 6 as a side dish

6	tablespoons olive oil
½	Spanish onion, thinly sliced
2	teaspoons salt
2	medium russet potatoes, peeled and sliced into thin rounds (about 3 cups)
5	large eggs, beaten
2	tablespoons heavy cream
1	teaspoon fresh thyme leaves

TORTILLA de CALABAZA

BUTTERNUT SQUASH OMELET WITH FRIED SAGE

Prepare the tortilla as directed, but substitute ½ medium butternut squash, peeled, seeded, and sliced into thin rounds (about 3 cups) for the potatoes (or try sweet potatoes, sunchokes, or parsnips; this version is also a great outlet for leftover roasted veggies). Omit the thyme and garnish the tortilla with fried sage leaves: Heat ¼ cup olive oil in a small saucepan over medium-high heat. Gently drop 1 sage leaf into the hot oil; it should immediately float to the top and the oil should bubble on the surface. If not, heat the oil a little longer. Once the oil is hot enough, fry 6 to 12 nice sage leaves until crispy and lightly browned, about 30 seconds. Using a slotted spoon or skimmer, transfer to a paper towel to drain. Salt lightly while still warm. Top each serving of tortilla with a fried sage leaf or two.

TORTILLA de CHORIZO

POTATO AND CHORIZO OMELET

Prepare the tortilla as directed, but omit the thyme and add 2 tablespoons Chorizo Vinaigrette (see page 58) or minced dry-cured chorizo (or ground or thinly sliced jamón, or rendered bacon lardons) to the egg-and-potato mixture before pouring it into the pan.

HUEVOS ROTES

"CRASHED" EGGS

VERDE

AMARILLO

ROJO

We highlighted our take on *rotos* in the introduction (see page 6) because, in many ways, it demonstrates our approach to Spanish cooking—we transformed a simple Spanish staple into an interesting, but most of all satisfying, modern dish. Breaking completely from tradition, we've also created dozens of seasonal rotos recipes, our favorites of which are included in the following pages. Ramps, local wild onions, are harbingers of spring in the east that annually incite hysteria among chefs and diners; they inspired our first vegetarian rotos. Carrots are a farmers' market standby that help us bridge the gap between several other variations; the creamy Carrot Vinaigrette (page 61) coats the potato strands in a way that may be even more reminiscent of spaghetti carbonara, the Roman pasta dish, than its classic, chorizo-laced rotos counterpart.

ROTOS ROJOS

POTATO STRANDS, CHORIZO VINAIGRETTE, AND SLOW-POACHED EGG

The vinaigrette here is terrific in a number of other applications (including the chorizo tortilla on page 54). Make lots and keep it on hand: Let cool and store in a tightly covered jar in the fridge for up to 2 weeks.

To make the vinaigrette, cut the chorizo into 8 chunks. Transfer to a food processor and pulse until finely ground.

In a frying pan over low heat, warm the olive oil with the chorizo and cook gently for 5 minutes, stirring occasionally. Add the onion, garlic, and thyme leaves, and continue cooking on low heat until the onion has practically melted into the chorizo oil, about 20 minutes longer. Remove from the heat and stir in the vinegar. Set aside.

To make the Rotos potatoes:

Using a Benriner turning slicer (spiralizer) with a medium cutter insert (see Note), turn the potato to create long strands. Hold in cold water until you're ready to fry. Pour oil into a deep fryer or heavy-bottomed pot to a depth of 4 inches and heat to 375°F. Just before the oil comes to temperature, poach the eggs (see the box on page 61). When the oil is hot, drain the potatoes thoroughly and pat dry. Carefully add to the hot oil and fry for about 8 seconds—just long enough to slightly cook the potatoes, but leaving them a bit crunchy. Using a slotted spoon or skimmer, transfer to a large bowl lined with paper towels to drain as much oil as possible.

Remove the paper towel, add a sprinkle of salt, 6 tablespoons of the vinaigrette, the chopped parsley, and vinegar. Mix thoroughly to coat the potato strands.

Divide the potatoes among four shallow bowls and shape each into a nest to rest the egg in. Place an egg in the middle of each nest, sprinkle with a bit of salt, and serve immediately.

NOTE: *Turning slicers (or "spiralizers," as they're often known) have become a popular kitchen gadget because they help create pasta-like noodles from vegetables, which are therefore gluten-free. They function a bit like a rotating mandoline slicer and similarly often have differently sized blades that can be used to create a variety of different shapes and sizes. You can find them online and in kitchen-supply stores.*

Serves 4

For the Chorizo Vinaigrette:

- 4 ounces cured chorizo (we use Palacio brand, the spicy version)
- ¼ cup olive oil
- 2 tablespoon finely diced onion
- 2 cloves garlic, minced
- Leaves from 2 sprigs fresh thyme
- 2 tablespoons sherry vinegar

- 1 large russet potato, peeled
- Canola oil for frying
- 4 large eggs
- Salt
- 1 tablespoon chopped fresh flat-leaf parsley
- 1 teaspoon sherry vinegar

ROTOS VERDES

POTATO STRANDS, RAMP SALSA VERDE, AND SLOW-POACHED EGG

If you can't find ramps for the salsa, you can substitute pretty much anything green (scallion tops, turnip tops, kale), but add ½ clove of raw garlic before blending. To dress the dish up even more, you could grate some aged Manchego (or other hard cheese) over the top, or lay a few paper-thin slices of jamón on the egg.

To make the salsa verde, bring a small saucepan of water to a boil. Salt it heavily—it should taste of the sea. Prepare an ice bath by filling a large bowl with equal parts ice and water. Add the ramp tops and parsley to the boiling water. Blanch for 20 seconds. Using a spider or slotted spoon, quickly transfer to the ice bath. Let cool, then drain, squeezing most of the liquid out (a little remaining water is fine). Chop the ramps and parsley coarsely.

In a blender, combine the blanched greens, lemon zest, and 2 tablespoons water from the ice bath. Blend to a smooth paste, then slowly drizzle in the olive oil. Taste for salt and add some, if needed. Set aside. (The salsa will keep, in an airtight container in your fridge, for up to 2 days.)

Make the potatoes as described in the Rotos Rojos recipe (page 58) and the eggs as described in the note opposite.

While the oil is heating, get a sauté pan (preferably cast-iron) ripping hot over high heat. If the ramps are bulbous, which happens at the end of the season, cut the bottom few inches in half, leaving the ramps intact but split on the bottom, which will allow them to cook similarly to younger ramps. Add the olive oil and ramps to the hot pan. Place a weight (if you don't have a grill weight, another pan or small pot will do) on top of the ramp bottoms to increase the contact they are making with the pan and help them char uniformly. When nicely charred on the first side, after about 90 seconds, flip and repeat on the other side for about 30 seconds. Season with salt and transfer to a bowl. Cover the bowl tightly with plastic wrap to allow the ramps to steam and tenderize and keep warm.

After draining the fried potato strands, add a sprinkle of salt, then the charred ramps, salsa verde, lemon juice, and parsley. Mix thoroughly to coat the potato strands.

Divide the potatoes among four shallow bowls and shape each into a nest to rest the egg in. Place an egg in the middle of each nest, sprinkle with a bit of salt, and serve immediately.

Serves 4

For the Ramp Salsa Verde:

Salt

12 ramps, green tops only (save the bottoms for pickling or another use)

1 small bunch fresh flat-leaf parsley

Zest of ½ lemon

3 tablespoons olive oil

1 large russet potato, peeled

Canola oil for frying

4 large eggs

12 ramps, roots trimmed, cleaned (you can substitute thin scallions or thicker scallions cut in half lengthwise)

1 teaspoon olive oil

Salt

1 tablespoon chopped fresh flat-leaf parsley

1 teaspoon fresh lemon juice

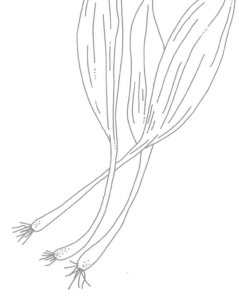

ROTOS AMARILLOS

POTATO STRANDS, MARINATED CARROTS, AND SLOW-POACHED EGG

You can make this colorful, earthy, and tangy vinaigrette ahead; let cool and refrigerate in a tightly covered jar for up to 4 days. You can also use the vinaigrette to create a salad dressing with deep flavor; make as directed, then thin out a little with more oil and vinegar to the consistency you like. Note that you need to make the Marinated Carrots at least a few hours ahead of time.

To make the vinaigrette, bring a small saucepan of water to a boil. Salt it heavily—it should taste of the sea. Add the carrots and garlic to the boiling water, reduce the heat to a simmer, and cook for 8 to 12 minutes, until the carrots are fork-tender. Using a spider or slotted spoon, transfer the carrots and garlic to a blender (you can use a colander to drain, but be sure to save some of the cooking water). Add 2 tablespoons of the cooking water, the olive oil, vinegar, thyme, a pinch of salt, and a few cracks of pepper. Blend until smooth. Taste and adjust the seasoning. Set aside.

Make the potatoes as described in the Rotos Rojos recipe (page 58) and the eggs as described in note below.

After draining the fried potato strands, add a sprinkle of salt, then the vinaigrette, parsley, and sliced marinated carrots. Mix thoroughly to coat the potato strands.

Divide the potatoes among four shallow bowls and shape each into a nest to rest the egg in. Place an egg in the middle of each nest, sprinkle with a bit of salt, and serve immediately.

Serves 4

For the Carrot Vinaigrette:

Salt

½   pound carrots, peeled and cut into 1-inch chunks (about 2 cups)

1   large or 2 small garlic cloves

3   tablespoons olive oil

1   tablespoon sherry vinegar

1   teaspoon fresh thyme leaves

Freshly ground black pepper

1   large russet potato, peeled

Canola oil for frying

4   large eggs

Salt

1   tablespoon chopped fresh flat-leaf parsley

6   pieces Marinated Carrots (page 44), cut on a bias into slices about 1 inch long

SLOW-POACHED EGG

IF you have an immersion circulator, cook the eggs at 144.5°F (62.5°C) for approximately 45 minutes. This technique is great for making a large quantity of poached eggs at once, rather than having to poach eggs one-by-one.

IF you are poaching eggs traditionally, bring a pot with at least 6 inches of water to a simmer and add salt and a splash of white vinegar. Crack an egg into a small bowl or container and then using a large spoon, stir the simmering water to create a vortex in the center of the pot. Gently tip the egg into the vortex and cook until the white is set. Carefully remove with a slotted spoon.

MiGAS

CRUMBS

When I was studying abroad in Madrid, my favorite class was taught by a British expat who had married a Spaniard and had lived in Spain for some thirty-plus years. His perspective, still somewhat that of an outsider, made his observations about Spanish culture particularly enlightening and his—shall we say—healthy appetite proved he had sampled much of the local cuisine. The highlight of the class was a weekend trip to visit his country house in the Sierra de Gredos mountains, a few hours outside Madrid. Passed down from his wife's family, their diminutive stone cottage within a small community of farmers and shepherds, nestled in a picturesque valley, felt as though it had been untouched by time.

It was on this trip, in a neighboring town large enough to have a restaurant (which my host's town was not) that I first sampled migas. That first taste was migas in its simplest, purest form: a fried egg and some chunky bread crumbs fried in olive oil, some pork scraps, and a healthy dose of pimentón. While nothing remarkable, it reminded me of one of my favorite meals of the year—breakfast the day after Thanksgiving: a fried egg over a pile of crispy leftover sausage stuffing.

That plate of migas was my first exposure to a dish that is served all over Spain as a method of repurposing leftovers. (Though, as described in Matt Goulding's terrific *Grape, Olive, Pig*, in the poorest villages in Spain, migas were made by slowly toasting and stirring flour and oil over a fire until pebble-like crumbs formed, rather than starting with bread.) Pretty much every cuisine has a few of these quasi-recipes in its repertoire, but they rarely make it onto restaurant menus. Unless you are invited to eat in a local's home, they're easy to miss.

While making the crumbs takes some time, you can't use storebought crumbs here because they are far too fine; on the other hand, storebought croutons are likely to be too large.

Preheat the oven to 300°F.

If the bread has a dark crust, trim off some or all of it, else the crumbs may be bitter. Brush the bread with the oil. Place the bread slices on a baking sheet, ideally on a wire rack so that both sides can toast evenly, and toast for 15 to 20 minutes. They won't have picked up much color, but the toast should be completely dried out (you should be able to split them in half by hand). Let cool slightly, then break up the bread as much as possible by hand, or use a knife to cut each slice into a few pieces.

Place the toasted bread pieces in a sturdy bowl and use a smaller bowl or a small pot to crush them into irregular crumbs that vary in size but are roughly between the size of a caper and a pea. The migas can be stored in an airtight container at room temperature for several weeks.

NOTE: *Just as there are often a few hunks of bread leftover after a meal, when you cut perfect portions of meats or fish, and even vegetables, for one dish, you're likely to end up with some trim. That trim is often just as tasty, but esthetically less pleasing. Chop up that trim, toss it with some crumbly croutons, serve it with an egg . . . and suddenly looks don't matter.*

8   slices day-old baguette
(or 4 slices of a larger loaf)

3   tablespoons olive oil

MIGAS CON GUISANTES Y JAMÓN

FRIED EGGS WITH PEAS, SPANISH HAM, AND CRUMBS

If you happen to keep frozen peas on hand, this is a perfect "pantry dish"—that is, one you may well have all the ingredients for without a trip to the grocery store. It's exceedingly simple to make and satisfying to eat. We use the butts of jamón—the pieces that are too small or irregular to slice—but you could use any cured ham, such as prosciutto or country ham, or really any pork product, like bacon, sausage, smoked ham, or roast pork. By all means use fresh peas if they're in season, but frozen peas do just fine.

Warm a sauté pan over medium heat for 1 minute. Add the olive oil and garlic. Toast the garlic, stirring, for 30 to 45 seconds, then add the jamón and onion. Sweat for 5 or 6 minutes, until the onions are translucent. There should still be a good deal of fat in the pan—the initial oil, plus a bit of fat rendered from the ham.

Add the peas and Migas Crumbs. Toss until the peas are warmed through and the crumbs have soaked up any remaining fat. Add the parsley and season with salt and black pepper. Add the acid—lemon juice for a lighter, fresher finish or sherry vinegar for something a bit heartier with a sweeter finish. Remove from the heat and set aside while you cook the eggs.

Fry the eggs in a little butter, as we do in the States, or in olive oil like the Spanish (either way, about 2 tablespoons). I like them sunny-side up. Season the eggs with salt and black pepper, and a pinch of red pepper flakes, if you like.

To serve, divide roughly half of the crumb mixture among four plates or shallow bowls. Place an egg (or two) on top of the mix and then spoon the remaining crumbs over the egg, leaving the yolks exposed. If you want to gild the lily, grate some cheese over the top. Serve immediately.

Serves 4 as breakfast, lunch, or part of a larger dinner

- **2** tablespoons olive oil
- **2** cloves garlic, thinly sliced
- **½** cup diced jamón
- **½** medium yellow onion, finely diced
- **2** cups fresh or frozen peas, blanched (see page 72)
- **1½** cups Migas Crumbs (page 62)
- **1** tablespoon chopped fresh flat-leaf parsley

    Salt and freshly ground black pepper

- **1** teaspoon fresh lemon juice or sherry vinegar
- **4 to 8** eggs (depending on whether you want to serve 1 or 2 per guest)

    Butter or olive oil for frying

    Red pepper flakes for sprinkling (optional)

    Manchego, Parmesan, or other hard, sharp cheese for serving

MIGAS CON PIPERRADA

FRIED EGGS WITH PEPPERS, BACON, AND CRUMBS

Basque sauces are legendary, and among the most famed is *piperrada*. As with any classic, every grandmother in the region has her own recipe. Peppers, onions, and garlic are always at the core, while tomatoes usually join the mix. Piperrada is often served with a fried egg and jamón. We like to use bacon—the smokiness works perfectly with the sweet roasted peppers—and the crumbs add texture and soak up the yolk in the same way a side of toast would. The moves we think make our piperrada a cut above the rest are collecting the juices released from the peppers after roasting and adding those to the sauce, and finishing that sauce with aged sherry vinegar, which is made from Pedro Ximénez grapes and has a round and nuanced flavor.

To make the piperrada, preheat the oven to 450°F. On a large baking sheet, toss the bell peppers and the cubanelle pepper, if using, with 1 tablespoon of the olive oil and season with salt. Spread the peppers apart on the pan and roast for 20 minutes, or until the skins are nicely charred on all sides, turning once or twice as needed. (You can char the skins more quickly under the broiler or by grilling them; however, I discourage this, as roasting for a longer time makes them sweeter and more tender.) Remove the peppers from the oven and transfer to a bowl. Cover the bowl tightly with plastic wrap and set aside to cool.

While the peppers are cooling, in a sauté pan over medium-high heat, combine the remaining 2 tablespoons olive oil, the onion, and the garlic and cook, stirring occasionally, until the onion begins to brown and char slightly. Add the thyme and season with salt and pepper. Pour in the wine and deglaze the pan, scraping up any browned bits from the pan bottom. Stir briefly until the wine has evaporated. Remove from the heat and set aside.

Unwrap the bowl of peppers and peel them, working over the bowl to capture all of the juices trapped inside the peppers and from the condensation in the bowl. Discard the stems and seeds and slice the peppers. Add the peppers to the onion mixture in the sauté pan and return to medium-high heat. Strain the pepper juices left in the bowl to remove any seeds and skins, and add the juice to the pan. Simmer until the liquid is reduced by half, then stir in the vinegar. Taste and adjust the seasoning. (At this point, you can store the piperrada, in an airtight container in the refrigerator, for up to 3 days.)

To season the crumbs, combine the olive oil, garlic, and thyme in a cold frying pan. Heat over medium heat for 3 minutes, stirring the garlic while it toasts. Add the Migas Crumbs and toast, stirring often, for 3 minutes. Season with salt and remove from the heat. Once cool, pick the garlic clove and thyme sprigs out of the crumbs and discard. Set the crumbs aside.

Place a sauté pan over medium heat and add the olive oil and the bacon. Cook the bacon until crisp, 3 to 5 minutes (depending on how crispy you like your bacon). With the bacon fat remaining in the pan, add the piperrada and the cherry tomatoes and cook, stirring just until everything is warmed through. Season with salt and pepper. Remove from the heat and set aside while you fry the eggs.

Fry the eggs in a little butter or olive oil (either way, about 2 tablespoons). I like them sunny-side up. Season with salt and pepper.

To serve, divide the eggs among four plates. Spoon one-fourth of the piperrada onto each plate, over the eggs. Finally, scatter or pile the seasoned crumbs over the plate, dividing them evenly. (I usually prefer to concentrate the crumbs in one area, so that diners can control how crunchy each bite is.)

Serve immediately.

Serves 4 as breakfast, lunch, or part of a larger dinner

For the Piperrada:

2 red bell peppers

1 yellow bell pepper

1 cubanelle pepper (optional)

3 tablespoons olive oil

   Salt and freshly ground black pepper

1 yellow onion, thinly sliced

3 cloves garlic, thinly sliced

1 teaspoon chopped fresh thyme

½ cup dry white wine

1 tablespoon Pedro Ximénez vinegar or other aged sherry vinegar

For the crumbs:

1 tablespoon olive oil

1 clove garlic, lightly crushed

2 sprigs fresh thyme

1 cup Migas Crumbs (page 62)

   Salt

1 teaspoon olive oil

4 ounces bacon, diced

8 cherry tomatoes, halved

   Salt and freshly ground black pepper

4 to 8 eggs (depending on whether you want to serve 1 or 2 per guest)

   Butter or olive oil for frying

MIGAS CON GARBANZOS, MORCILLA Y ESPINACA
FRIED EGGS WITH CHICKPEAS AND BLOOD SAUSAGE

This is almost certainly the migas recipe that you are least likely to make at home—but it may well be my favorite, and is too tasty to omit. Blood sausage is not easy to find, especially the mild Asturian morcilla that we make. Look for it at Spanish specialty foods stores, or quality butcher shops. If you can't find blood sausage (and because it's not up everyone's alley), you can substitute fresh chorizo, butifarra, or another pork sausage.

To season the crumbs, in a cold frying pan, combine the olive oil, garlic, and thyme. Heat over medium heat for 3 minutes, stirring the garlic while it toasts. Add the Migas Crumbs and toast, stirring often, for 3 minutes. Season with salt and remove from the heat. Once cool, pick the garlic clove and thyme sprigs out of the crumbs and discard. Set the crumbs aside.

In a blender, combine 1 tablespoon of the olive oil, ½ cup of the chickpeas, and ½ cup of the chickpea cooking liquid. Process to a smooth purée. Season with salt and pepper and set aside.

In a sauté pan over medium heat, heat the remaining 1 tablespoon olive oil. Add the morcilla and cook until warmed through, using a wooden spoon to crumble it as it cooks. Add the remaining 2 cups chickpeas and remaining ½ cup cooking liquid. Bring to a simmer. Stir in the chickpea purée to thicken the mix. Add the spinach and stir just until wilted, 1 minute or less. Season with the vinegar and salt and pepper.

Fry the eggs in a little butter or in olive oil (either way, about 2 tablespoons). I like them sunny-side up. (Poached eggs are also great for this dish.) Season with salt and pepper.

To serve, divide the eggs among four plates. Spoon the morcilla mixture over the eggs. Finally, scatter or pile the seasoned crumbs over the plate, dividing them evenly. (I usually prefer to concentrate the crumbs in one area, so that diners can control how crunchy each bite is.) Serve immediately.

Serves 4 as breakfast, lunch, or part of a larger dinner

For the crumbs:

1	tablespoon olive oil
1	clove garlic, lightly crushed
2	sprigs fresh thyme
2	cup Migas Crumbs (page 62)
	Salt

2	tablespoons olive oil
2½	cups cooked chickpeas
1	cup chickpea cooking liquid (if using canned beans, substitute chicken stock or water)
	Salt and freshly ground black pepper
½	pound precooked morcilla sausage, casings removed
2	cups loosely packed baby spinach
2	teaspoons Pedro Ximènez sherry vinegar or other aged sherry vinegar
4 to 8	eggs (depending on whether you want to serve 1 or 2 per guest)
	Butter or olive oil for frying

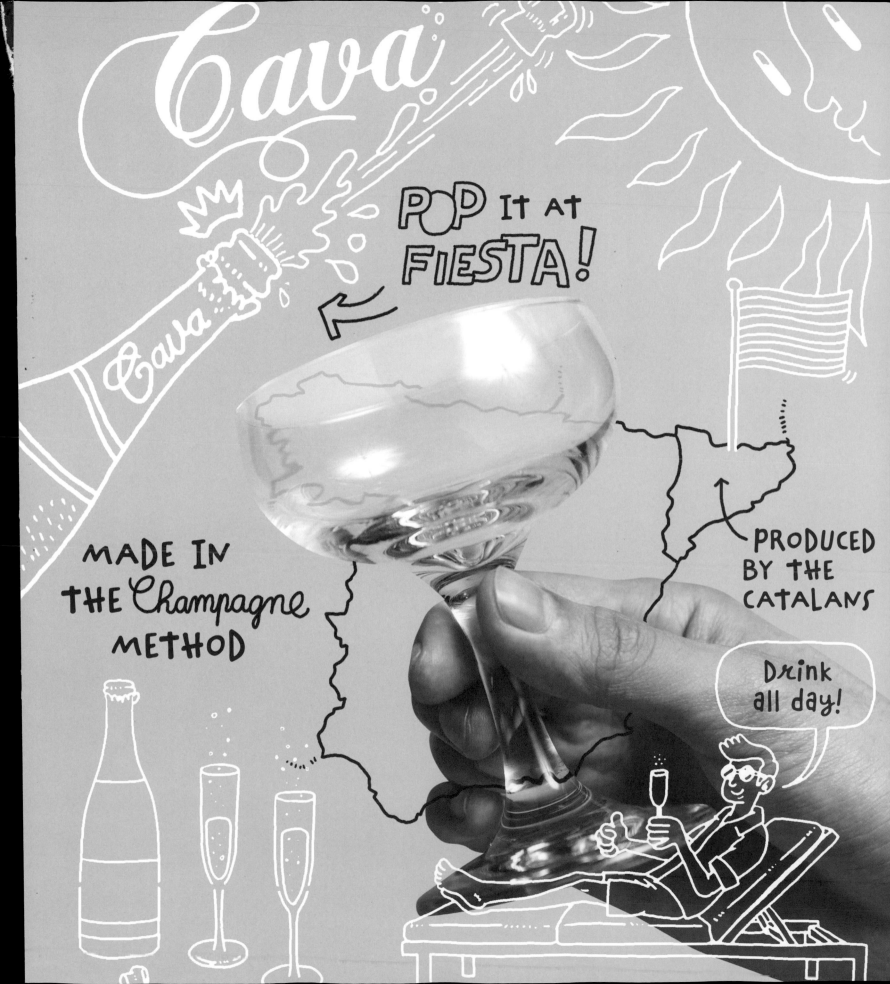

Basque Brunch

BEVERAGE PAIRING

AGUA DE VALENCIA
& CERVEZA SANGRE

ROLLOS DE PEPINO CON TRUCHA
24

MANCHEGO CON MEMBRILLO
30

MIGAS CON PIPERRADA
64

HUEVOS ROTOS
58

PATATAS BRAVIOLI
80

JAMÓN SERRANO

TORRIJAS
189

Brunch as a concept is uniquely American. Luckily for us and our late-morning guests, many of Spain's most familiar dishes can be enjoyed at any time of day. In fact, besides breakfast, which is generally little more than a coffee and toast or pastry, Spaniards' diets don't change much throughout the course of the day. There isn't a culture of quick and portable midday food—lunch is often the largest (and longest) meal of the day in Spain. Tapas and pintxos, which are usually eaten in the early evening, are also enjoyed in the late morning, particularly on weekends—somewhat analogous to our brunch.

Creating a Basque brunch was not so challenging, as many of our dinner menu offerings already seem more like something you'd expect to eat early in the day: eggs, potatoes, sausages, and smoked fish. Furthermore, the classic light wine and beer cocktails, part of a loose category we call *refrescos*, make the perfect pairing for a midday meal.

REVUELTOS

SCRAMBLED EGGS

IF YOU FIND THE IDEA of eating eggs after breakfast to be disconcerting, then scrambled eggs will likely be the biggest hurdle to cross. In Spain, where breakfast tends to be light, eggs are eaten at any time of day or night. Carefully scrambled eggs with just a few ingredients folded into the mix can make an elegant start to a dinner or, accompanied by a salad, a perfect lunch.

Revueltos con Camarones
Scrambled Eggs with Shrimp

Adding shrimp goes a long way towards separating scrambled eggs from the breakfast table. That's not to say that you shouldn't eat shrimp for breakfast, but shrimp certainly elevate a humble scramble. The texture and flavor of this dish remind me of a somewhat lighter shrimp and grits, and to that end, a little ham or bacon would be a nice addition, just as they are in the Southern classic.

In a large bowl, beat the eggs with the cream and season conservatively with salt and pepper.

In a large nonstick frying pan, melt the butter over medium heat. Add the scallion whites and cook, stirring often, until translucent, about 2 minutes. Add the egg mixture and, using a rubber spatula, stir constantly. To help curds form, you can let the eggs cook for 15- to 30-second intervals without stirring, but to keep those curds small, you do want to stir often.

When the eggs are about half-cooked, but still quite runny—with curds just beginning to form—remove from the heat and stir in the shrimp and crème fraîche. Return to medium heat and cook, stirring gently, until you've achieved a soft scramble. It should only take another minute or two. If you prefer your eggs cooked further, cook them for a minute or two longer.

Divide the eggs among four bowls and top with the sliced scallion greens. If using the shrimp oil, drizzle ½ teaspoon over the top (see Note). Serve immediately, with toast on the side.

NOTE: *If you would like to make shrimp oil to drizzle over the eggs, which both looks nice and reinforces the shrimp flavor, it's quite simple: Heat 1 cup olive oil in a small saucepan over medium heat. Add 1 cup shrimp shells and 3 cloves garlic, crushed, and let it all toast in the hot oil for 5 to 7 minutes, stirring occasionally. Remove from the heat and add 1 bay leaf and 1 teaspoon sweet or hot pimentón and let the oil steep for at least 30 minutes and up to 3 hours. Strain the oil through a fine-mesh strainer. You can store the oil, refrigerated, for several weeks.*

Serves 4 as breakfast, lunch, or part of a larger dinner

10	large eggs
½	cup heavy cream
	Salt and freshly ground black pepper
2	tablespoons unsalted butter
6	scallions, sliced into thin rounds, white bottoms and green tops separated
½	pound large shrimp (21-25 count), peeled (save the shells to make shrimp oil for drizzling, if you like; see Note), deveined (see page 148), and cut in half
1	tablespoon crème fraîche or sour cream
	Crusty bread slices, toasted, for serving

REVUELTOS DE PRIMAVERA
SPRING SCRAMBLE

Bring a small saucepan of water to a boil. Salt the water heavily (about 1 tablespoon kosher salt for every 2 cups water). Prepare an ice bath by filling a large bowl with equal parts ice and water.

Add the English peas to the boiling water and blanch until tender-crisp; frozen peas will only need about 30 seconds, while fresh will take longer. Using a slotted spoon, immediately transfer to the ice bath. Next blanch the snow peas and then the snap peas until tender-crisp, transferring them to the ice bath as soon as they're done. Each type should take 2 to 3 minutes, but taste-testing is always best. Drain all of the peas and pat dry.

In a large bowl, beat the eggs with the cream and season conservatively with salt and pepper. Heat a large sauté pan over medium-low heat. Melt the butter, add the olive oil and all of the peas, as well as the egg mixture and the cheese. Using a rubber spatula, stir constantly. To help curds form, you can let the eggs cook for 15- to 30-second intervals without stirring, but stir often until you've achieved a soft scramble. It should only take about 3 minutes. If you prefer your eggs cooked further, cook them for a minute or two longer. Taste and adjust the seasoning.

Divide the eggs among four bowls. Garnish with the pea shoots, if using. Serve immediately, with toast alongside.

Serves 4 as breakfast, lunch, or part of a larger dinner

Salt and freshly ground black pepper

1 cup English peas, fresh or frozen

1 cup snow peas, strings removed

1 cup snap peas, strings removed

10 large eggs

½ cup heavy cream

1 tablespoon olive oil

2 tablespoons unsalted butter

2 tablespoons grated Manchego cheese

1 handful pea shoots (optional)

Crusty bread slices, toasted, for serving

REVUELTOS CON CHAMPIÑONES Y QUESO
SCRAMBLED EGGS WITH MUSHROOMS

Preheat a large nonstick frying pan over medium-high heat for 2 to 3 minutes. Add the olive oil, leeks, and mushrooms. (Cook in two batches or two pans if needed to avoid crowding the pan.) Sauté for 5 to 7 minutes, stirring occasionally, until the mushrooms have taken on some color and become tender. Season with salt and pepper, then stir in the thyme. Cook for 1 more minute.

Meanwhile, in a large bowl, beat the eggs with the heavy cream and season conservatively with salt and pepper. Reduce the heat under the mushrooms to medium-low and add the butter and the egg mixture. Using a rubber spatula, stir constantly. To help curds form, you can let the eggs cook for 15- to 30-second intervals without stirring, but stir often.

When the eggs are about half-cooked, but still quite runny—with curds just beginning to form—remove from the heat and crumble in the goat cheese. Return to medium heat and cook, stirring gently, until you've achieved a soft scramble. It should only take another minute or two. If you prefer your eggs cooked further, cook them for a minute or two longer. Taste and adjust the seasoning.

Divide the eggs among four bowls and serve immediately. Bread might be nice . . .

Serves 4 as breakfast, lunch, or part of a larger dinner

2 tablespoons olive oil

1 leek, white part only, sliced thinly

1 small handful each cremini, oyster, and hen of the woods mushrooms, wiped clean with a damp towel and cut into roughly ½-inch chunks

Salt and freshly ground black pepper

1 teaspoon chopped fresh thyme

10 large eggs

½ cup heavy cream

2 tablespoons unsalted butter, at room temperature

2 tablespoons goat cheese

SHOOTS

ENGLISH

Peas

SNOW

SNAP

VEGETALES

IT IS NOT EASY being a vegetarian in Spain. Even as an omnivore, I find that dining out and looking for a respite from all the jamón can prove difficult. What makes this all the more frustrating is that if you've had the chance to visit one of the countless markets in whatever city or town you find yourself, beautiful produce is abundant. Upon closer examination, you begin to find delicious and simple dishes that elsewhere might be categorized as "sides" hidden as tapas in Spain. It's not unlikely that they are laced with pork or cheese or at the very least saturated with olive oil by the time they reach your table, but we've adapted many of the classics to provide a fresher take.

"Spanish Kimchi"

CRUDITÉS WITH WHITE ANCHOVY–PIMENTÓN DIP

It is sometimes debated whether cooking is an art. I'm not sure where I stand on the subject, but any good cook, like many an artist, keeps notebooks filled with ideas. It was in one of my notebooks that I discovered an entry I had written years earlier that simply said, "Spanish Kimchi. Boquerones. Pimentón. Sherry Vin." I knew what to do from there; I just needed to stumble upon it at the right time. That right time was a day when I also had a couple heads of beautiful Caraflex cabbage on hand and no plan for them. Initially we marinated the cabbage as you would treat napa cabbage in traditional kimchi, but each time I made a batch, I would snack on the freshly dressed cabbage, and at some point it hit me that our version (which is not fermented) was actually better before sitting for days (or weeks).

Pulse the scallions and garlic together in a food processor until coarsely chopped. Add the boquerones (and their marinade), vinegar, sugar, salt, and sweet and hot pimentóns and pulse until a rough paste forms. The dip can be used immediately, or refrigerated, tightly covered, indefinitely.

Arrange the vegetables on a platter and serve with the dip.

Makes 1 pint; serves 8 to 12

- 6   scallions, white parts only
- 6   cloves garlic
- 6   ounces (about ¾ cup) boquerones (white anchovies) and their marinade
- ⅓   cup sherry vinegar
- 2   tablespoons sugar
- 1   tablespoon salt
- 2   teaspoons sweet pimentón
- 1   teaspoon hot pimentón

  Raw vegetables cut into bite-sized slices or sticks for serving (we like carrots, radishes, young turnips, and small, crispy heads of cabbage or lettuce cut into wedges)

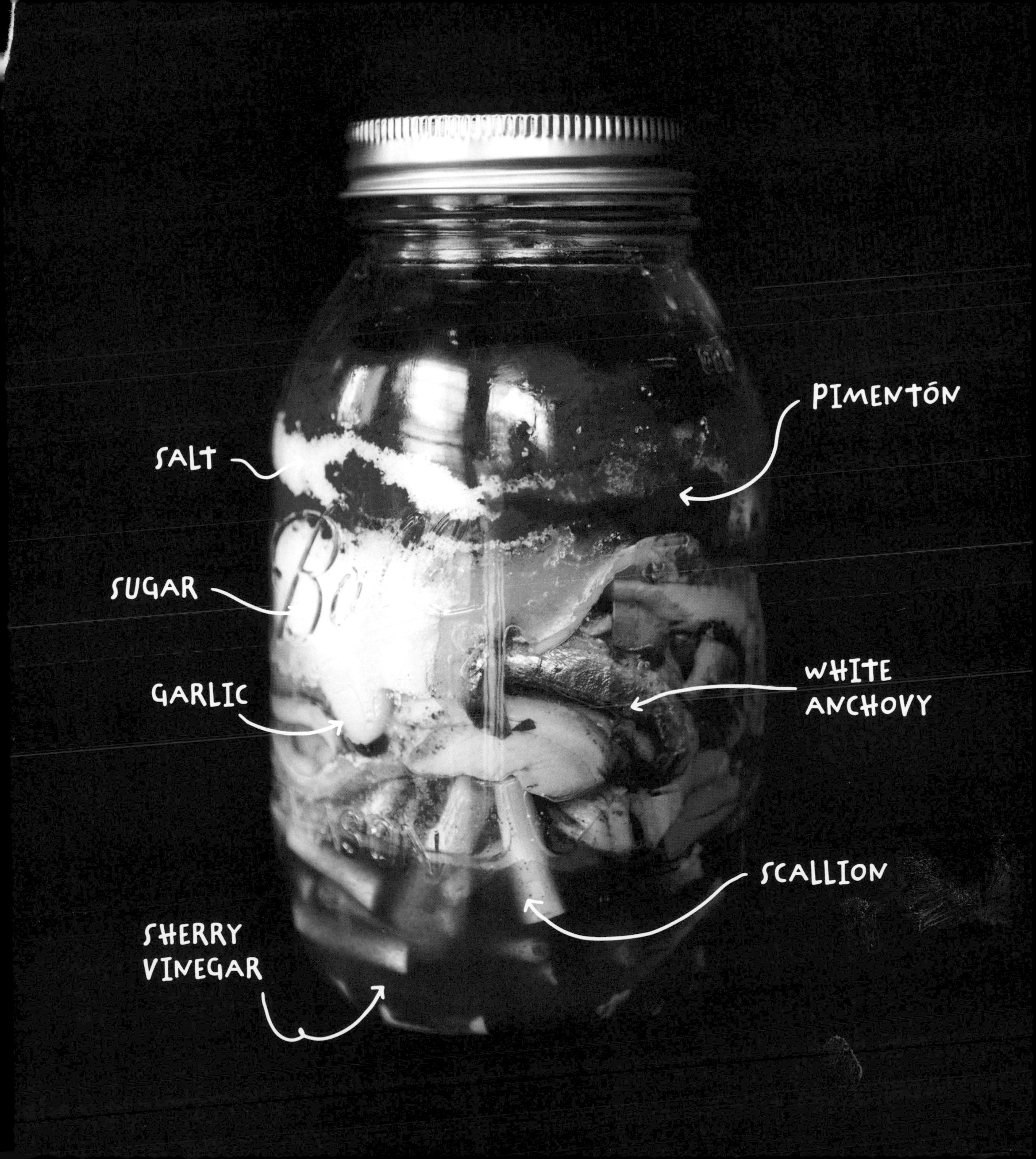

PIMENTÓN

SALT

SUGAR

GARLIC

WHITE
ANCHOVY

SCALLION

SHERRY
VINEGAR

DEEP-FRY
TOMATOES FOR
30 SECONDS to
POP THE SKIN
AND PEEL

SALMOREJO

GAZPACHO'S SOUTHERN COUSIN

TOMATO AND BREAD SOUP WITH HARD-BOILED EGG AND JAMÓN

While it's hard to argue with gazpacho, in the interest of introducing our guests (and yours) to something a little different, we prefer to serve *salmorejo*—gazpacho's heartier southern cousin. A chilled tomato soup, salmorejo includes a good deal of bread as a thickener and is usually served garnished with hard-boiled eggs and diced jamón, making it a rather substantial summer soup.

Salmorejo is traditionally served in a *cazuela*, an earthenware dish, which is usually used for hot dishes as it holds the heat well, but in this case, it helps maintain the dish's chill.

Heat 1 tablespoon of the olive oil in a sauté pan over medium heat. Add the onion and stir to coat in the oil. Cook until the onion begins to color, stirring occasionally to prevent burning or sticking. When it's taken on a little color, reduce the heat to low and continue to cook very slowly, stirring often, until caramelized to a rich, deep golden brown, about 30 minutes total. If you find that the onion is sticking at any point, sprinkle in a tablespoon or so of water, and use your spoon to scrape up any browned bits that are stuck to the pan bottom. Remove from the heat and let cool.

Combine the peeled tomatoes, garlic, bread, caramelized onions, water, vinegar, thyme, salt, and remaining 1 cup olive oil in a large bowl. Toss, breaking the tomatoes up and making sure that the bread begins to absorb the liquids and soften. Let sit at room temperature for 30 minutes, stirring periodically, at which point the bread should be saturated.

Transfer the soup to a blender and blitz on high speed until smooth and silky. If you find that the mixture is too tight (it should be thick for a soup, but you shouldn't struggle to blend it), add up to 1 cup additional water, working in small increments. Taste and adjust the seasoning. In addition to more salt, depending on the acidity of your tomatoes you may want to add more vinegar. Cover and chill in the refrigerator for at least 2 hours and up to 3 days.

Spoon a thick layer (about 1½ inches) of soup into each of four individual *cazuelas* (see recipe introduction) or shallow bowls. Garnish with the hard-boiled egg, jamón, chives, and a drizzle of olive oil and serve immediately.

NOTE: *We like to peel tomatoes by tossing them in the fryer (see opposite). But here's how to peel tomatoes the conventional way: Using the tip of a paring knife, score the bottom of the tomatoes with a small "x." Plunge the tomatoes into boiling water for 30 seconds and then into an ice bath. Once cool, the skins should peel off with relative ease.*

Serves 4 as a part of a larger meal

1	tablespoon plus 1 cup olive oil, plus more for drizzling
1	medium yellow onion, thinly sliced
1	pound tomatoes, peeled (see Note)
1	small clove garlic, lightly crushed
10	slices baguette (about ½ inch thick), cut into quarters
1	cup water (if your tap water isn't tasty, use bottled)
2	tablespoons Pedro Ximénez sherry vinegar or other aged sherry vinegar
1	teaspoon fresh thyme leaves
1	tablespoon salt, plus more to taste
2	hard-boiled eggs, peeled and quartered
½	cup finely diced jamón
1	tablespoon minced fresh chives

PATATAS BRAVIOLI

FRIED POTATOES WITH BRAVAS SAUCE AND AÏOLI

It's hard to go wrong with fried potatoes. Patatas Bravioli is the marriage of two classic preparations, *patatas bravas* and *patatas alioli*. *Bravas* is sort of a Spanish ketchup, and aïoli (*alioli* in Spanish) is a garlicky mayonnaise-based sauce that many people favor with their fries. *Patatas bravas* translates to roughly to "fierce [or spicy] potatoes," or, more artfully, "potatoes with a temper." In reality, the sauce is more smoky (from the pimentón) than hot. This speaks to a point that sometimes surprises some of our guests—Spanish food is seldom spicy.

As is the case with nearly any recipe that requires frying, you could instead roast the potatoes (tossed in oil) in a hot oven to make the dish a bit healthier and avoid the fuss of setting up a fryer (see Note).

To make the Bravas Sauce, heat the 1 tablespoon olive oil in a frying pan over medium heat. Add the onion and cook, stirring often, until it turns a deep golden brown. Move the onion to one side of the pan and add the 1 teaspoon olive oil and the smashed garlic. Allow the garlic to toast for 1 minute, stirring. Add the pimentón and oregano, allowing the spices to bloom in the warm onions and garlic. Season with salt and then deglaze the pan with the vinegar, using a wooden spoon to scrape up any browned bits from the bottom of the pan. Using your hands, crush the plum tomatoes into the pan with their juices. Add the *piquillo* peppers. Reduce the heat to maintain a simmer and cook gently for 30 minutes, stirring occasionally. Taste and add salt, if needed. Remove from the heat and let cool for 30 minutes. Transfer to a blender and buzz at high speed until a ketchup-like consistency is achieved.

To make the Aïoli, whisk all the ingredients together in a bowl until well blended and smooth.

To prepare the potatoes, just as when making a good french fry, the best approach is to "blanch" the potatoes in moderately hot oil before finishing them in hot oil. Pour oil into a deep fryer or heavy-bottomed 4-quart pot to a depth of 4 inches and heat to 300°F. Using a skimmer or slotted spoon, add the potatoes to the oil and fry for about 5 minutes, until they are fork-tender. Transfer to paper towels to drain, but do not season. Let cool for at least 5 minutes while you raise the oil temperature to 375°F. When the oil has reached temperature, carefully return the potatoes to the hot oil and fry until golden and crispy, about another 4 minutes. Drain and season with salt.

To serve, either spoon the sauces over the warm potatoes, or serve alongside for dipping.

NOTE: *To roast the potatoes instead of frying, preheat the oven to 400°F. On a baking sheet, toss the potatoes in olive oil and salt and spread in a single layer. Roast until golden and crispy, about 15 minutes.*

Serves 4 as part of a larger meal

For the Bravas Sauce:

1	tablespoon plus 1 teaspoon olive oil
½	yellow onion, thinly sliced
1	large or 2 small garlic cloves, smashed
1½	teaspoons hot pimentón
1	teaspoon chopped fresh oregano
	Salt
2½	cups canned whole peeled plum tomatoes in their juice
1	cup stemmed and thinly sliced piquillo peppers
3	tablespoons sherry vinegar

For the Aïoli:

2	cups Hellmann's mayonnaise (we love Hellmann's, and we're not afraid to admit it!)
1	large or 2 small cloves garlic, grated on a Microplane
1	teaspoon fresh lemon juice
1	tablespoon olive oil
1	teaspoon salt

For the fried potatoes:

	Canola oil for frying
3	large russet potatoes, peeled and cut into irregular 1-inch chunks
	Salt

PIRIÑACA

CUCUMBERS, TOMATO, ONION, TUNA CONFIT, AND HARD-BOILED EGG

You don't see much lettuce in Spain. When you do, often it's tight wedges from small lettuce heads, and you could certainly add some of those to this salad. But more often salads are chock-full of tomatoes and peppers—two New World ingredients that have become integral to Spanish cooking. Very often hard-boiled eggs are added and tuna or *boquerones* are used as a finishing touch. There's nothing more to it, but you could certainly add any number of other ingredients: sliced fennel bulb, radishes, olives, and other "soft" herbs like tarragon, dill, or chervil.

Bring a small pot of water to a boil and using a spoon, gently lower the eggs into the water. Boil for 9 minutes and remove the eggs, placing them in an ice bath. When cool enough to handle, peel the eggs and cut them into quarters.

Remove the bell pepper stem and seeds and cut the pepper into thumb-sized planks. If you are using cherry tomatoes, simply cut them in half. If you are using larger tomatoes, cut them as you please. Place all the vegetables in a large bowl and add the parsley. Drizzle in 5 tablespoons of the olive oil and the vinegar and season with salt and pepper. Toss lightly, so as not to destroy the tomatoes.

Gently transfer the salad to a platter rather than a bowl, so that the tomatoes don't get crushed, and also so you can arrange the tuna and eggs evenly over the top. After placing the eggs and tuna on the dressed veggies, hit them with some salt and pepper. Drizzle the remaining 1 tablespoon olive oil over the top. Serve immediately.

Serves 4

- 4 large eggs
- 1 yellow or orange bell pepper (or any other color)
- 1 pound tomatoes (the best you can find)
- 2 Kirby cucumbers, peeled and sliced into thin rounds
- ½ cup fresh flat-leaf parsley leaves
- 6 tablespoons olive oil
- 2 tablespoons red wine vinegar

    Salt and freshly ground black pepper
- 8 ounces best-quality canned tuna, drained and flaked (see page 42 to make your own)

ASADiLLO

PIQUILLO PEPPERS, GEM LETTUCE, PICKLED ONION, SMOKED TROUT, AND OLIVES

We're always excited to introduce guests to *sidra*, Spanish cider, so we themed our first menu "The Asturian Cider House" (you'll find a version of it in this book on page 137). Nate once had a memorable meal at Casa Mingo, an Asturian cider house in Madrid, that included *asadillo*—a hearty dish of roasted *piquillo* peppers, onions, canned tuna, hard-boiled eggs, and olives. In our re-creation, we added diminutive Gem lettuce leaves to create a lighter salad; pickled the onions to add some acid and crunch; and replaced the tuna with smoked trout.

We like to serve this salad with the Tortilla Española (page 52) and bread on the side.

Trim the base of the lettuce heads and gently separate the leaves. Keeping the leaves whole, wash them and dry thoroughly.

Get a pan ripping hot; add 1 teaspoon of the olive oil and then the piquillo peppers. Char on the first side for 2 minutes, then flip. Sear for 1 minute on the second side, then remove from the heat and deglaze the pan with the vinegar, using a wooden spoon to scrape up any browned bits from the pan bottom. Season with salt and black pepper and transfer to a bowl or plate, along with any vinegar that hasn't evaporated or been soaked up by the peppers.

Flake the smoked trout into 10 to 12 pieces. Tear each piquillo into 2 or 3 pieces.

In a bowl, dress the lettuce with the remaining ½ cup olive oil, the lemon juice, and any sherry vinegar left behind in the piquillo bowl. Season with salt and black pepper.

To finish, in a large serving bowl or deep plate, thoughtfully compose the salad. Lay some lettuce down, followed by a few chunks of egg, trout, piquillo peppers, olives, and onions. Repeat, layering the ingredients until you've used them all. Serve immediately.

Serves 4

2	heads Little Gem lettuce or any baby lettuce heads
1	teaspoon plus ½ cup olive oil
10	canned or jarred piquillo peppers
1	tablespoon Pedro Ximénez sherry vinegar or other aged sherry vinegar
	Salt and freshly ground black pepper
12	ounces smoked trout, store-bought or homemade (page 39)
2	teaspoons fresh lemon juice
5	soft-boiled (simmered for 6 to 7 minutes) eggs, peeled and quartered lengthwise
½	cup meaty black olives, such as Empeltre or Kalamata, pitted
½	cup Pickled Red Onions (see page 45)

BATATAS CON MOJO PICÓN
SWEET POTATOES WITH MOJO PICÓN SAUCE

While we primarily look to the north of Spain for inspiration, it is indeed a large country with many regional cuisines. The cooking in the south has stronger Moorish and Jewish influences, making some of the methods and seasonings more akin to cooking in North Africa and the Middle East—regions that are increasingly inspiring chefs around the world. *Mojo picón* is a sauce from the Canary Islands, a Spanish archipelago off the west coast of Africa. There it is traditionally served with *papas arrugadas* ("wrinkled potatoes"), which are cooked in seawater; we use our mojo instead as a dressing for sweet potatoes, an ingredient you are more likely to find in Africa than Spain. The sweet potatoes benefit from the smoky pimentón and earthy cumin, as would grilled meat or fish of almost any kind.

Preheat the oven to 400°F.

Cut the potatoes into large (about 1½-inch) chunks. Toss them in a bowl with the olive oil and season with salt and black pepper. Roast for 30 minutes, or until fork-tender and lightly browned. If they are tender but haven't taken on any color, you can turn your broiler on high and broil them for 1 or 2 minutes.

While the potatoes are roasting, make the sauce: Put the cumin and coriander seeds in a dry sauté pan over medium heat. Toast them, stirring constantly, until their fragrance intensifies, 3 or 4 minutes. Grind the toasted seeds in a spice grinder (a coffee grinder that you only use for spices) or crush them in a mortar using a pestle (If you don't have either of those tools available, you can just buy ground spices and skip the toasting step.)

In a small saucepan, heat the olive oil over medium heat. Add the pimentón and ground cumin and coriander. Allow the spices to "bloom" in the oil, which further intensifies their flavor. Stir for 15 seconds and remove from the heat. Be careful; if your oil is too hot, you will burn the spices. Let cool slightly, then transfer the oil and spice mixture to a bowl.

Using a Microplane grater, grate the garlic into the bowl. Chop the almonds coarsely by hand and add them to the bowl along with the oregano, vinegar, and salt. Stir to mix well. (The mojo will keep, tightly covered in the fridge, for 1 week or more, but the flavors may become less intense.)

To serve, put the roasted sweet potatoes in a large bowl. Spoon the mojo over the potatoes and mix well. Arrange on a platter and garnish with the goat cheese, pumpkin seeds, and parsley. Serve immediately.

Serves 4 as a part of a larger meal

- **3** sweet potatoes (any variety will work), scrubbed
- **2** tablespoons olive oil
- Salt and freshly ground black pepper

For the Mojo Picón Sauce:
- **2** teaspoons cumin seeds
- **1** teaspoon coriander seeds
- **⅔** cup olive oil
- **⅓** teaspoon hot pimentón
- **1** small clove garlic
- **⅓** cup almonds
- **1** teaspoon chopped fresh oregano
- **2** teaspoons sherry vinegar
- **1** teaspoon salt
- **3** tablespoons crumbled goat cheese
- **2** tablespoons toasted pumpkin seeds (pepitas)
- **¼** cup fresh flat-leaf parsley leaves

CANARY ISLANDS

Setas al Ajillo

MUSHROOMS WITH GARLIC

Spaniards love garlic—go to a tapas bar anywhere in Spain and you're bound to find a handful of *al ajillo* dishes—where garlic is the main seasoning. Mushrooms too are a favorite, particularly in the north of Spain. There's not much more to this dish—usually a handful of parsley, a bit of salt, maybe some lemon, and of course plenty of olive oil. We've served mushrooms and garlic in many forms: quickly sautéed and finished with grated raw garlic; roasted and dressed with a smoked garlic vinaigrette; and cooked in duck fat with a raw egg yolk on top.

Wipe the mushrooms with a damp towel to clean. Cut the creminis into quarters, or sixths if they are very large. Cut the trumpet mushrooms in half; if using shiitakes, leave the caps whole or cut in half if they are very large. Pull the hen of the woods into thumb-sized pieces.

Preheat a large sauté pan over high heat for 2 minutes. (If your pan isn't large enough to cook all the mushrooms in a single layer without crowding, cook them in two batches or two pans. If you do the latter, it makes sense to cook the different types of mushrooms separately and combine them after.) Add the garlic oil and turn the heat down to medium-high. Add the trumpet mushrooms and cook, cut-side down, for 2 minutes. Add the remaining mushrooms and the fresh sliced garlic. Let the mushrooms cook for 6 to 8 minutes, stirring occasionally. If they have absorbed all the oil and the pan is dry, add a bit more garlic oil. They should have some color at this point; season with salt and deglaze the pan with the sherry, using a wooden spoon to scrape up any browned bits from the pan bottom. Let the alcohol cook out and then stir in the Garlic Confit and parsley.

Serve immediately, with lemon wedges on the side.

Serves 4 as a part of a larger meal

- ½ pound cremini mushrooms
- ½ pound trumpet royale or shiitake mushrooms
- ½ pound hen of the woods or maitake mushrooms
- 2 tablespoons garlic oil (see page 18)
- 4 cloves garlic, thinly sliced
-    Salt
- ½ cup amontillado (or other dry) sherry, or white wine
- 10 cloves Garlic Confit (see page 18)
- 3 tablespoons chopped fresh flat-leaf parsley
-    Lemon wedges for serving

PIMIENTOS DE PADRÓN

BLISTERED PADRÓN PEPPERS

Whenever I see Padrón peppers on a menu, I order them. They are so easy to prepare that they say little about the talent in the kitchen, but do speak to the restaurant's ability to source product well. Too often shishito peppers, which are tasty in their own right, are served in their place; while they're a reasonable substitution, they just aren't the same. Padróns have thinner skins, making them less bitter and more tender than shishitos. Both peppers are occasionally quite hot—it's often said that one in ten are spicy, making eating a plate with a group of friends a low-risk game of Russian roulette. Oftentimes someone who substitutes shishitos for Padróns thinks that it's the preparation—blistering the skin of the small green peppers in a hot pan or fryer—that makes them "Padrón peppers," rather than the variety. Padróns are named for the town of their origin, located in Galicia in the northwest of Spain, a town I've had the pleasure of visiting.

In much of Spain, particularly the rural areas, there is still a strong tradition of "market days," where residents from the surrounding areas—many from hours away—descend on a town that is hosting a large market. Twice a month, the small town of Padrón hosts the largest market in Galicia.

On one trip, my wife and I decided to visit Padrón. We arrived around 9:30 a.m., and already the town was teeming. We followed the locals' lead and pulled our rental car over just before reaching the diminutive exit ramp, parking and walking the rest of the way; there were no parking spots left in town. As we approached the center of the market, we found most of the men huddled under a large tent, drinking the local beer, Estrella Galicia, and devouring plates of *pulpo a la gallega* (see page 154). The women were catching up with friends as well, but did so as they shopped, stall to stall, stocking up on *tetilla*, chorizo, mussels, and, of course, the famed local peppers.

It felt as if anywhere we stood within the hundreds of vendors, we could spot a giant basketful of peppers. Almost as frequently we would find an elderly woman hunched over the basket, or seated with a basket on her lap, separating the peppers. Somehow, perhaps from the weight, they seem to be able to pick the spicy Padróns from the lot, eliminating unwelcome surprises for their faithful patrons.

Alas, Padróns aren't so plentiful back home in the States, but they are starting to crop up. I've found them at farmers' markets, both at home in New York and around California, and at the restaurant we're fortunate to have a wine purveyor of Gallegan descent whose parents grow Padróns in their New Jersey backyard, many of which find their way to our kitchen—so I can only hope that you'll be able to find some, too. And, at the end of the day, shishitos can be treated in just the same way . . . they just aren't quite the same.

Get a cast-iron pan ripping hot. If you don't have cast-iron, use your heaviest sauté pan. If you can fit all the peppers in the pan in one layer, add all of the olive oil and peppers. If you can only fit half the peppers without crowding, cook in two equal batches.

Once the peppers are in, if you have a grill weight, use it to press the peppers to the pan bottom; alternatively, use another pot or pan as a weight.

Adjust the heat to medium-high and char the peppers on the first side for 2 to 3 minutes. Remove the weight and stir the peppers around so that the majority are now flipped over. Cook for another 2 minutes, stirring occasionally. The skins should be blistered and the peppers somewhat softened. Season generously with sea salt and transfer to a serving dish.

You can serve the peppers with a couple lemon wedges for squeezing over the top, or you may prefer them straight up. A little bread on the side is a good idea, not just for mopping up the excess oil, but in case you get a hot one!

**Serves 4 as a part
of a larger meal**

½ pound (about 4 cups)
Padrón peppers

2 tablespoons olive oil

Maldon or other sea salt

Lemon wedges for serving
(optional)

Baguette for serving (optional)

ESPÁRRAGOS CON ALMENDRAS Y QUESO

ASPARAGUS WITH ALMONDS AND RONCAL

As you'll find with most recipes in this chapter (with the exception of saladlike preparations), our approach to vegetables is typically not to combine them, but rather let them all play a starring role, with techniques, seasonings, and flourishes that highlight or complement their flavors and textures.

You can certainly roast or grill the asparagus here, but because the almonds, Roncal, and mustard are all assertive flavors, we usually opt for the milder results from blanching the asparagus.

Trim the woody ends of the asparagus stalks by gripping them, one at a time, with one hand at the very bottom of the stalk and one in the middle. Bend until the end snaps off, letting it break where it will naturally. It's usually about one-fourth of the way up the stalk. If the asparagus are very thick, you can peel off the outer skins with a vegetable peeler to tenderize them.

Fill a pot large enough to hold the asparagus either vertically or horizontally three-fourths full of water and bring to a simmer over high heat. Salt the water heavily; it should taste of the sea.

Next, add the asparagus to the seasoned, simmering water and, depending on the thickness of the stalks, simmer for 1 to 3 minutes. The best way to tell if they are done is to taste-test one; they should still have some snap to them and remain bright green. Drain the asparagus. Pat the stalks dry and transfer to a platter large enough to spread the asparagus in a single layer.

In a bowl, whisk together the olive oil, vinegar, lemon juice, and mustard. Don't worry about slowly adding the oil, as there's no need to emulsify this vinaigrette. Season with salt and pepper.

To finish, spoon the vinaigrette over the plated asparagus and top with the almonds and grated cheese. Serve immediately.

Serves 4 as a part of a larger meal

- 1   pound asparagus

  Salt and freshly ground black pepper
- 2   tablespoons olive oil
- 2   tablespoons aged sherry vinegar
- 1   tablespoon fresh lemon juice
- ½   teaspoon Dijon mustard
- 2   ounces Roncal or Manchego cheese, grated
- 2   tablespoons Marcona almonds, chopped

PARTY MENU

CATALÁN CALÇOTADA

ESPÁRRAGOS CON
ALMENDRAS Y QUESO
88

BUTIFARRA

CALÇOTS CON ROMESCO
94

CORDERO A LA PARRILLA
131

MEL I MATÓ
184

BEVERAGE PAIRING
ROSÉ CAVA

There is perhaps no more famous feast in Spain then the *calçotada*. Named for the famed calçots, or "overwintered" onions, this annual gathering draws huge crowds to the countryside of Catalunya. It's hard to imagine so much fervor for a vegetable. Maybe for a mushroom or truffle . . . but the excitement caused by this onion variety is nearly unfathomable—imagine hundreds of thousands of Americans traveling each year to a corner of the country to eat a regional specialty, and a vegetable nonetheless! But, just like so many Spanish delicacies, it's as much about the party surrounding the food as the food itself.

The mild onions, similar to scallions, are planted in the spring for what usually would be a fall harvest, but instead are left in the ground until the following spring. Growers pile extra dirt around the shoots during this period to cultivate a larger portion of the tender white section. In spring, they are the perfect size—similar to small leeks—to be charred over an open fire, then peeled and dunked into the addictive romesco sauce of the region. As luck would have it, the timing aligns with the availability of spring lambs, which also happen to work well on the grill.

This meal is best enjoyed outdoors, where you can more comfortably get your hands and cheeks messy, particularly when guzzling wine straight from a *porrón* (a glass carafe with a very narrow spout that evolved from the practice of drinking wine from sheep or goat bladders)—which certainly adds to the youthful exuberance.

CALÇOTS CON ROMESCO

CHARRED SPRING ONIONS WITH ROMESCO SAUCE

I was first introduced to this feast not in the Catalan countryside, but rather the streets of New York. For twenty years, chef Peter Hoffman set up a large grill on SoHo's Crosby Street outside his restaurant Savoy for an annual *calçotada*. As a nineteen-year-old cook there, I got my first taste of this terrific tradition.

The technique may seem foreign to most cooks—allowing the onions to burn to the point where they appear inedible—but the preparation is fairly simple and the results are remarkably satisfying. What is more difficult is finding onions that mimic the calçots that are harvested in Spain. While you might find onions in this state at your local farmers' market in early spring, you likely will be forced to find a suitable alternative later in the year. We find that very fat scallions or spring onions whose bulbs haven't begun to form will work, but thin leeks are really your best bet.

Make sure you have plenty of newspaper, butcher paper, or parchment paper and a cooler on hand before you begin your calçotada.

Not only is this a dish to eat outside, but even more so, it's a dish to cook outside. It can be done in your broiler, but it's not the same. Set up a grill, preferably with lump hardwood charcoal, and get it quite hot; the fire needs to be hot enough to burn the outer layer of the leeks quickly without turning the interior to mush.

No need to clean the leeks before cooking them; any sand in or on them will either burn off or will peel off with the burnt skin. Lay the leeks on the grill so that the whites are over the hottest part and the green tops are either over a low heat or, ideally, are hanging off the side of the grill.

Allow the leeks to cook for 3 or 4 minutes, or until they have completely charred and blackened on one side. Using long tongs, turn them over and allow the other side to char. When the leeks are completely blackened, transfer them in groups of 5 onto sheets of newspaper. Wrap them tightly in the newspaper. Next, transfer the bundles of wrapped leeks to a cooler or other insulated container. Alternatively, you can wrap each bundle in plastic wrap. This will allow the leeks to steam and become tender. Let them steam and cool for about 30 minutes.

Put out the Romesco Sauce in a bowl or bowls for dipping. To serve, unwrap the bundles as needed. Simply snip the root ends off the leeks, cutting off both the roots and about ¼ inch of the white; this will allow for easy peeling. Holding the uncharred green tops, your guests can then peel off the burnt layer. Dip the leek whites into the romesco—and next, lower them dramatically into your wide-open mouth!

Serves 4 as a part of a larger meal

20   thin leeks (or calçots, if you have them—see recipe introduction)

Romesco Sauce (page 141), processed until smooth, for serving

BRÓCOLI CON ANCHOAS

BROCCOLI WITH ANCHOVIES

I love broccoli. Yet it seems to have been relegated to the ranks of a "pedestrian" vegetable and is seldom seen on the menus of ambitious restaurants or on the pages of creative cookbooks. It is incredibly versatile—as at home with melted Cheddar as it is with fish sauce—and when thoughtfully cooked, its tender crunch is craveable. Its flavor is mild, so we love to use small doses of potent ingredients as condiments to add depth and a punch.

This is a dish that may seem to want acid. Depending on my mood, or what else I'm eating, I might add a squeeze of lemon juice, or use pickled chile peppers instead of fresh.

Preheat the oven to 425°F.

If you have a very large, ovenproof sauté pan, big enough to fit all the florets in a single layer, heat that on the stovetop over medium heat for 3 minutes. If you don't have a pan that large, place a baking sheet in the oven for 10 minutes. (Preheating not just the oven but also the baking sheet will increase the likelihood of achieving a pleasing char.)

While the pan is preheating, in a large bowl, toss the broccoli with 2 tablespoons of the olive oil and season with salt. Dump the broccoli into the preheated pan or baking sheet and roast in the oven for 12 to 16 minutes. The timing will depend a bit on how large your florets are—ideally the broccoli is charred on one side, still fairly bright green on the remaining sides, and just tender in the middle.

While the broccoli roasts, make the sauce: Chop the anchovies into fingernail-sized pieces (use 4 or up to 6, depending on how much you like anchovies). Set aside. In a small pan over medium-low heat, combine the remaining 2 tablespoons olive oil and the garlic. Toast the garlic, stirring, until the edges are lightly browned, about 1 minute. Add the chile and cook for 1 more minute. Remove from the heat and stir in the anchovies. Cover the sauce to keep warm and set aside.

When the broccoli is done, transfer to a serving bowl and toss with the anchovy sauce. Serve immediately, or let the broccoli marinate and the flavors intensify, and serve at room temperature. (This dish is great cold the next day as well; just give it a few minutes to warm up so any oil that has congealed can liquefy slightly.)

Serves 4 as a part of a larger meal

2	heads broccoli, cut into florets
4	tablespoons olive oil
	Salt
4 to 6	olive oil–packed anchovies
2	cloves garlic, thinly sliced
1	red finger chile or Serrano, sliced as thinly as possible (taste a tiny piece; if it is very spicy or you are sensitive to spice, you may want to remove the seeds)

COLIFLOR CON ALIOLI DE AZAFRÁN

ROMANESCO WITH SAFFRON AÏOLI

As Thanksgiving nears in New York, our farmers' markets become increasingly sparse, with the exception of squash and root vegetables. During this time of year, I always look forward to the beautiful varieties of cauliflower that remain in season. My favorite among them is Romanesco—in part because its dramatic fractal pattern and chartreuse color make it look like something out of a Dr. Seuss book. But I also find the stems and leaves to be tastier than those of your standard cauliflower.

To make the aïoli, combine the wine and saffron in a small saucepan and bring to a simmer over medium heat. Remove from the heat and let steep for at least 20 minutes. When the wine is bright yellow and cooled to room temperature, transfer to a bowl. Add the mayonnaise, garlic, olive oil, and salt and whisk until smooth. Set aside.

Cut the cauliflower into quarters, top to bottom. Now that the core is exposed, cut the core out of each quarter. If there are still leaves attached to the base of the core, cut them off and reserve them. Cut the core pieces into slices about ½ inch thick, discarding the bottom 2 inches or so of the stalk, which can be very tough. Set the core slices aside. Next, cut the cauliflower quarters into thumb-sized florets. Because the structure of Romanesco is tighter than most cauliflower, you will end up with less "natural"-looking florets and have more cut edges. This works in your favor, because there are more flat surfaces to caramelize while cooking.

Heat a large sauté pan over high heat. (If you can't fit all the cauliflower in a single layer without crowding, you will need to cook it in two batches or two pans.) Turn the heat down to medium-high and add the olive oil and all of the cauliflower. Cook, untouched, for about 5 minutes.

Give the pan a shake to turn the pieces. Add the garlic and any reserved leaves and cook for another 2 to 3 minutes, until the garlic is lightly toasted. Season with salt and black pepper and, if you like, a pinch of red pepper flakes. Pour in the wine and deglaze the pan, using a wooden spoon to scrape up any browned bits from the pan bottom. Turn the heat down to medium-low and cover the pan with a lid. Cook about 5 minutes longer to allow the cauliflower to steam and become tender. Remove the lid and taste a piece—it should be tender but not soft or mushy. Adjust the seasoning, if necessary. Let cool for a few minutes before serving.

To serve, spread a few spoonfuls of the aïoli on a large plate. Arrange the Romanesco over the top, in one layer so that every piece will get some sauce, but leaving some of the aïoli visible. Alternatively, serve the aïoli on the side. Serve warm (but this is also terrific at room temperature).

Serves 4 as a part of a larger meal

For the Saffron Aïoli:

- 2 tablespoons dry white wine
- ½ teaspoon saffron threads
- 2 cups good-quality mayonnaise (we love Hellmann's)
- 1 large or 2 small cloves garlic, grated on a Microplane
- 1 tablespoon olive oil
- 1 teaspoon salt

- 1 head cauliflower, any variety but preferably Romanesco
- 3 tablespoons olive oil
- 4 cloves garlic, thinly sliced
  Salt and freshly ground black pepper
  Red pepper flakes (optional)
- 1 cup dry white wine

Coliflor con
Alioli de Azafrán

CALABACÍN AL HORNO

GOLD BAR SQUASH, MARCONA ALMONDS, AND MANCHEGO

Vegetables dishes baked with a bread-crumb topping are found in all Mediterranean cuisines. This version highlights two of Spain's most iconic ingredients—Marcona almonds and Manchego cheese—and gets a bit of a lift from mint and lemon zest. Gold Bar is our favorite variety of summer squash, but zucchini or any other summer squash would do just fine. Try to find ones that aren't too large; 5 inches long and about 1½ inches thick is ideal.

Some anchovies draped over the top of these as well wouldn't be a bad idea!

In a bowl, combine the bread crumbs, almonds, cheese, garlic, parsley, mint, lemon zest, 1 teaspoon of the salt, and 1 tablespoon of the olive oil. Stir to mix well. Set aside.

Position an oven rack about 4 inches from your broiler and preheat the broiler to medium (or high, but not low). Line a baking sheet with aluminum foil.

Wash the squash and trim off the very bottom and most of the stem of each, leaving about ¼ inch of stem still attached. Split the squash in half lengthwise. Get a sauté pan ripping hot. Add the remaining 1 tablespoon olive oil and the squash halves, cut-side down. Sear for 4 minutes, allowing the squash to char and nearly burn on the first side. Flip, season the charred sides with the remaining 1 teaspoon salt, and cook for 1 minute longer.

Transfer the squash to the prepared baking sheet with the cut sides, which are now charred, facing up. Scatter the bread-crumb mixture over the squash and press down gently to help the mixture adhere to the squash. Broil until the cheese has melted and the crumbs and almonds have taken on a deep golden brown, 3 to 5 minutes. Remove from the oven, season the warm squash with the lemon juice, and serve immediately.

Serves 4 as a side dish

½	cup plain dried bread crumbs
½	cup skinless Marcona almonds, ground (or sub another variety of skinless almond)
½	cup grated Manchego cheese
1	clove garlic, minced
1	1 tablespoon chopped fresh flat-leaf parsley
1	tablespoon chopped fresh mint
	Zest and juice of ½ lemon
2	teaspoons salt
2	tablespoons olive oil
3	Gold Bar squash or other summer squash, such as zucchini

Berenjenas Con Miel

EGGPLANT WITH HONEY

There may be no vegetable that benefits more from frying than eggplant. That's one of the reasons eggplant is often so much better in restaurants than at home. It's best fried, or cooked whole and charred almost to the point of burning—two methods that can be difficult to employ at home. It's counterintuitive, but frying yields the lightest results, as the rapid cooking minimizes how much oil (or other fats or liquids) can be absorbed by the porous vegetable.

This is a very tasty dish on its own, but any number of garnishes could be added—try chopped almonds, pickled onions, or pomegranate seeds. Our favorite way to serve eggplant and honey is simply on charred toast with goat cheese.

Slice the eggplants into rounds about ¾ inch thick, discarding the end pieces. (If you are using a large eggplant, first cut it lengthwise into quarters and then into 1-inch cubes.) In a bowl, salt the eggplant heavily and transfer to a colander. Place a heavy bowl (or a bowl with something heavy inside) on top to press the eggplant, and place the entire setup in the sink. Let stand for 1 hour. You should see a good deal of moisture being released—and with it, some of the eggplants' natural bitterness will also dissipate. Rinse the eggplant, drain well, and pat dry thoroughly with paper towels.

Pour oil into a deep fryer or heavy-bottomed 4-quart pot to a depth of 4 inches and heat to 375°F. Working in small batches so you don't crowd the pot, fry the eggplant until deep golden brown, 3 to 4 minutes. Using a skimmer or slotted spoon, transfer to paper towels to drain thoroughly. Test a piece to see if the eggplant needs any additional salt; since it was heavily salted earlier, it may be adequately seasoned. If it needs salt, sprinkle on while the eggplant is still warm.

Once all the eggplant pieces are fried, place in a large serving bowl. Add the parsley, honey, and vinegar and toss to mix. Add garnishes, if you like (see recipe introduction), and serve immediately.

Serves 4 as a part of a larger meal

———————

4   slender Japanese eggplants, or 1 Italian globe eggplant

Salt

Canola oil for frying

1   cup loosely packed flat-leaf parsley leaves

3   tablespoons honey

1   tablespoon sherry vinegar

ARROZ

RICE IS A CRUCIAL PART of Spanish culture. The Iberian Peninsula

has been conquered by numerous cultures throughout history, and arguably no invasion had a greater impact on the cuisine than the Moorish invasion. Chief among the Arabic ingredients they brought to Spain is rice; Spain is now the second-largest producer in the world. It is grown in a number of different parts of the country (with attached "Denominaciónes de Origen" much like wine) and cooked in numerous styles. Paella is certainly the most famed Spanish rice preparation; although we don't include a recipe for paella per se in this book (or on the restaurant menu), in this chapter we have featured several rice dishes that are prepared in a small paella pan in a very similar manner to the familiar saffron-spiked classic. Fideos, or noodles, are certainly second fiddle to rice in Spain, but have become an alternative in certain preparations, as well as finding their way into soups and the like, so we included one classic Spanish noodle dish.

ARROZ AL CHINO

SAFFRON FRIED RICE WITH BACON AND SHRIMP

In most countries around the world, it's hard to find many restaurants serving anything but the local cuisine. That's still largely the case in Spain, even in the capital, so when I studied abroad, I began to long for the diversity of New York. Then I discovered the Chinese restaurant located in an underground parking lot below the Plaza de España.

This favorite—inspired by my memories of Madrid's finest Chinese restaurant—is an amalgam of Spanish paella and Chinese fried rice. We chose not to serve paella at the restaurant, in part to avoid the stereotypical favorite dish of Spaniards, but also because it can be challenging to make well, given the constraints of our kitchen. Places that serve good paella tend to have kitchens that have been designed to cook paella. Ours is not (and neither is yours). Fried rice produces a crunchiness that replicates the *soccorat*, the crispy bottom layer, of great paella, and the shrimp and bacon—typical in Chinese fried rice—mimic the combination of shellfish and chorizo common in paella.

Line a baking sheet with parchment paper.

Cook the rice according to the package instructions, adding the saffron to the cooking water and also 1 tablespoon salt (if not called for). When the rice is done, turn it out onto the prepared baking sheet and spread in an even layer. Let dry in the refrigerator, uncovered, for at least 2 hours or preferably overnight.

Heat your largest sauté pan over high heat for 3 minutes. Turn the heat down to medium and add the canola oil, twirling the pan to disperse it, and then the rice, spreading it evenly over the bottom of the pan. Scatter all of the peas, the bacon, and the shrimp on top of the rice, but do not mix in. Allow the dish to cook undisturbed for 5 minutes, so that the rice toasts on the bottom and the ingredients on top steam to warm through (or in the case of the shrimp, become nearly cooked).

After 5 minutes, a nice crust should be formed on the bottom. If not, or if your rice isn't warmed through, stir gently and toast for 3 more minutes, then stir everything together until the ingredients are evenly distributed. If using pea leaves, add them now.

While the rice is finishing, in a small frying pan, melt the butter. Add the eggs and scramble to a medium-well done texture (large curds that won't completely fall apart when folded into the rice). Remove the rice pan from the heat and fold in the scrambled eggs, again distributing them evenly.

To serve, heap the rice on a large platter. If serving with Aïoli, either place the sauce in a squeeze bottle and squirt zigzags over the top, or simply serve in a small bowl on the side. Serve immediately.

Serves 4

1½	cups medium-grain rice
1	teaspoon saffron threads
	Salt
1	tablespoon canola or vegetable oil
1	cup English peas, fresh or frozen, blanched (see page 72)
1	cup snap or snow peas, blanched (optional; see page 72)
4	ounces bacon lardons (about ½ cup), cooked until crisp and drained
12	extra-large (26/30 count) shrimp (about ½ pound), peeled and deveined (see page 148)
1	cup pea leaves or shoots (optional)
1	teaspoon unsalted butter
4	large eggs, beaten
½	cup Aïoli (page 80) (optional)

Arroz a la Niçoise

SAFFRON FRIED RICE, WAX BEANS, TOMATOES, OLIVES, TUNA, EGG

Save for a few classics, nothing stays on our menu indefinitely. But there are fan favorites, like the saffron fried rice, that we like to reinvent seasonally. In New York, when summer produce begins to flood the farmers' markets, it's hard to not buy everything you can carry and figure out what to do with it afterwards.

This dish was conceived on a quick cab ride back from the Union Square market, sharing the backseat with the morning's haul. We repurposed the core ingredients—wax beans, tomatoes, olives, tuna, and egg—of the much-loved southern French Niçoise salad (France, of course, neighbors Spain), swapping out the potatoes for rice and omitting the lettuce, and built a rice dish for summer.

Line a baking sheet with parchment paper.

Cook the rice according to the package instructions, adding the saffron to the cooking water and also 1 tablespoon salt (if not called for). When the rice is done, turn it out onto the prepared baking sheet and spread in an even layer. Let dry in the refrigerator, uncovered, for at least 2 hours or preferably overnight.

Heat your largest sauté pan over high heat for 3 minutes. Turn the heat down to medium and add the olive oil and then the rice, spreading it evenly over the bottom of the pan. Scatter the blanched wax beans over the rice, but do not mix in. Allow the dish to cook undisturbed for 5 minutes, so that the rice toasts on the bottom and the beans on top steam to warm through. After 5 minutes, a nice crust should be formed on the bottom. If not, or if your rice isn't warmed through, stir and toast for 3 more minutes.

While the rice is toasting, in a small frying pan, melt the butter. Add the eggs and scramble to a medium-well done texture (large curds that won't completely fall apart when folded into the rice). Season with salt. Remove the rice from the heat and fold in the scrambled eggs, again distributing them evenly.

Return the pan to medium heat, add the tomatoes and olives, and cook, stirring, for 30 seconds. Back off the heat, stir in the lemon juice.

To serve, heap the rice on a large platter. Flake the tuna over the rice and scatter the onions over the top. If serving with Aïoli, either place the sauce in a squeeze bottle and squirt zigzags over the top, or simply serve in a small bowl on the side. Serve immediately.

Serves 4

1½	cups medium-grain rice
1	teaspoon saffron threads
	Salt
1	tablespoon olive oil
1½	cups wax beans, trimmed and blanched (see page 72)
1	teaspoon unsalted butter
4	large eggs, beaten
1	cup cherry tomatoes, halved
¼	cup meaty black olives, such as Empeltre or Kalamata, pitted
1	tablespoon fresh lemon juice
½	cup best-quality canned tuna, drained
¼	cup Pickled Red Onions (page 45)
½	cup Aïoli (page 80)

ARROZ CON CHAMPIÑONES

RICE WITH MUSHROOMS

While this recipe isn't a paella per se, it could certainly be confused for one. The technique is very much like making a paella, albeit a simple one; but the biggest practical difference is that paella is always the centerpiece of a meal, whereas this is a side dish—a complementary tapas-like portion—making it possible to cook over just a single burner.

This rice is the perfect accompaniment to any roast poultry or meat.

We've included a recipe for mushroom stock (see page 115), but while homemade stocks are almost always superior, you can certainly use storebought stock.

In a medium paella pan (about 10 inches) or a shallow sauté pan about the same size, combine 1 tablespoon of the olive oil, the onion, fennel, and garlic and sweat over medium heat, stirring occasionally, for 10 minutes. Add the remaining 1 tablespoon olive oil and the mushrooms, raise the heat to medium-high, and sauté for 3 or 4 minutes, until the mushrooms take on a little color and begin to release some liquid. Season with salt and add the thyme.

While the vegetables are cooking, pour the mushroom stock into a saucepan and bring to a simmer, then remove from the heat. Season the stock with salt; start with 1 teaspoon. The rice will be flavored and seasoned by absorbing the stock, so it's important that the stock is seasoned but not overseasoned, making the rice salty. If your stock tastes salty at any point while you're seasoning it, just add some water.

Add the rice to the pan with the diced mushrooms. Stir for 1 minute to toast. Pour in the sherry and deglaze the pan, using a wooden spoon to scrape up any browned bits from the pan bottom, and stir until the majority of the liquid has been absorbed. Using the back of the spoon, spread out the rice in the pan so it will cook evenly.

Add 2 cups of the mushroom stock, gently so as not to disturb the even layer of rice. (Unlike risotto, you don't stir the rice, so resist the temptation; this will allow a proper soccarat—the crispy bottom layer that is the mark of a perfect paella—to form.) Bring the stock to a simmer, then reduce the heat to medium and cook until the stock is mostly absorbed, about 5 minutes. Add another ladleful or two of stock (just enough to cover the rice again) and continue to simmer. Once you've added about 3 cups of stock total, taste the rice. It should be tender, with a little texture but not crunchy. If it is underdone, add some more stock, but not so much that it may overcook. (If the rice isn't done but seems on the edge of becoming oversalted, you can add warm water instead of more stock.)

When the rice has almost achieved the desired texture, stop adding stock and cook until all the remaining liquid is absorbed. Remove from the heat and let the rice cool and rest for 2 minutes.

To serve, scatter the Pickled Mushrooms over the top and sprinkle the chives over everything. Add a dollop of Aïoli on the top, or serve it on the side. Serve immediately.

Serves 4 as part of a larger meal

- 2 tablespoons olive oil
- 1 Spanish onion, finely diced
- ½ fennel bulb, finely diced
- 1 clove garlic, minced
- 8 ounces cremini mushrooms, brushed clean and cut into ¼-inch dice (about 1 cup) (save the stems for the stock, if making)
  Salt
- 1 teaspoon fresh thyme leaves
- 3 to 4 cups Mushroom Stock (page 115)
- 1 cup Calasparra, Bomba, or Arborio rice
- ½ cup dry sherry or white wine
- ½ cup Pickled Mushrooms (page 47)
- 1 tablespoon fresh chive batons (1-inch pieces)
- 2 tablespoons Aïoli (page 80)

Arroz con Zanahorias

RICE WITH CARROTS

This is a very similar recipe to the previous one, but while the technique is the same, the finished dish tastes entirely different. Whereas mushrooms are earthy and savory, carrots bring a light and sweet flavor to this rice, making it well matched for milder fare like Trucha a la Sal (page 172) and Pollo Asado (page 127).

In a medium paella pan (about 10 inches) or a shallow sauté pan about the same size, combine the olive oil, onion, carrots, celery, and garlic and sweat over medium heat, stirring occasionally, for 10 minutes. Season with salt and add the thyme.

While the vegetables are cooking, in a saucepan, combine the stock and juice. Bring to a simmer, then remove from the heat. Season the stock with salt; start with 1 teaspoon. The rice will be flavored and seasoned by absorbing the stock, so it's important that the stock is seasoned but not overseasoned, making the rice salty. If your stock tastes salty at any point while you're seasoning it, just add some water.

Add the rice to the pan with the vegetables. Stir for 1 minute to toast. Pour in the sherry and deglaze the pan, using a wooden spoon to scrape up any browned bits from the pan bottom, and stir until the majority of the liquid has been absorbed. Using the back of the spoon, spread out the rice in the pan so it will cook evenly.

Add 2 cups of carrot stock, gently so as not to disturb the even layer of rice. (Unlike risotto, you don't stir the rice, so resist the temptation; this will allow a proper soccarat—the crispy bottom layer that is the mark of a perfect paella—to form.) Bring the stock to a simmer, then reduce the heat to medium and cook until the stock is mostly absorbed, about 5 minutes. Add another ladleful or two of stock (just enough to cover the rice again) and continue to simmer. Once you've added about 3 cups of stock total, taste the rice. It should be tender, with a little texture but not crunchy. If it is underdone, add some more stock, but not so much that it may overcook. (If the rice isn't done but seems on the edge of becoming oversalted, you can add warm water instead of more stock.)

When the rice has almost achieved the desired texture, stop adding stock and cook until all the remaining liquid is absorbed. Remove from the heat and let the rice cool and rest for 2 minutes.

To serve, scatter the Marinated Carrots over the top of the rice and sprinkle the parsley leaves over everything. Add a dollop of Aïoli on the top, or serve it on the side. Serve immediately.

Serves 4 as part of a larger meal

1½	tablespoons olive oil
1	Spanish onion, cut into small dice
2	medium carrots, peeled and cut into small dice
1	small celery stalk, cut into small dice
1	clove garlic, minced
	Salt
1	teaspoon fresh thyme leaves
2 to 3	cups Carrot Stock (page 115)
1	cup carrot juice
1	cup Calasparra, Bomba, or Arborio rice
½	cup dry sherry or white wine
8 to 10	pieces Marinated Carrots (page 44)
1	tablespoon fresh flat-leaf parsley leaves
2	tablespoons Aïoli (page 80)

ARROZ MARINERO

SAILOR'S RICE

Before heading to Madrid for a semester, I was assigned to an apartment on Calle de las Huertas, in the heart of the historic Barrio de las Letras, so named because of the writers who once lived in the neighborhood. On one side of my building was the dwelling where Cervantes wrote *Don Quixote*, and on the other was a Gallegan restaurant called Maceiras. History aside, only one of these was a must-see for visiting friends and family.

Garishly decorated with buoys and fishing nets, the restaurant always had bagpipes playing over the sound system (Galician folk music, a holdover from the days when the Celts ruled the northwest of Spain). I sampled every dish on the menu over numerous visits. The one dish that cautioned a twenty-five-minute wait was the *arroz marinero*, a generous pot of soupy rice and seafood. It was worth the wait.

In a saucepan over high heat, bring the stock to a simmer and season lightly with salt. Reduce the heat to low.

In a large pot, heat the olive oil over medium-high heat for 1 to 2 minutes, until the oil begins to dance. Add the onion, bell pepper, and garlic. Stir and sweat for 3 minutes. Add the rice and toast, stirring, for 1 minute. Season with salt and add the pimentón and saffron, allowing them to bloom for several seconds. Pour in the wine and deglaze the pan, stirring with a wooden spoon to scrape up any browned bits from the pan bottom. Bring to a simmer and cook until reduced by half, about 5 minutes. Using your hands, crush the tomatoes and their juices into the pot.

Add the warm fish stock to the pan and reduce the heat to maintain a bare simmer. Cook, stirring occasionally, until the rice is nearly cooked, just a bit unpleasantly crunchy in the center, 12 to 16 minutes. Add the peas, cockles, and mussels, discarding any open shellfish that do not close to the touch. Cover the pot, and cook until the shellfish open, about 5 minutes. Discard any shellfish that fail to open.

Meanwhile, season the cod, squid, and shrimp with salt on both sides. When the shellfish has opened, add the cod, squid, and shrimp and stir gently, just so that they are submerged in the rice, not floating on the surface. Cook just until the shrimp are just pink and the cod begins to flake, 2 to 3 minutes longer.

Remove the pot from the heat and add the parsley and lemon juice. Stir gently. Taste and adjust the seasoning. Serve immediately, straight from the pot.

Serves 4

4	cups Fish Stock (page 115)
	Sea salt
2	tablespoons olive oil
½	Spanish onion, diced
½	green bell pepper, seeded and diced
1	clove garlic, minced
1½	cups Bomba, Calaspara, or Arborio rice
1	teaspoon sweet pimentón
½	teaspoon saffron threads
1	cup dry white wine
1	cup whole peeled canned tomatoes, with their juice
1	cup English peas, fresh or frozen
16	cockles (Manila or littleneck clams work equally well), scrubbed and purged (see page 38)
16	mussels, scrubbed and debearded
8	ounces squid, cleaned, bodies cut into thick rings
8	ounces cod, cut into 8 pieces total
8	large (21/25 count) shrimp (about ⅓ pound), peeled and deveined
3	tablespoons chopped fresh flat-leaf parsley
	Juice of 1 lemon

ARROZ NEGRO

BLACK RICE

There may be no people in the world as fond of eating ink as the Spaniards. Squid or cuttlefish ink is regularly used in cephalopod preparations—none more common than *arroz negre*. Here's a simple "black rice" enriched with squid ink and fish stock. It's delicious as is, but if you can get your hands on some squid, chop it into rings and add it to the rice with the last bit of stock. Serve with bread and lemon wedges and perhaps aïoli (see page 80), which is Spaniards' standard accompaniment for arroz negro.

Warm the fish stock in a pot over high heat. Season lightly with salt. Hold at a bare simmer.

Heat a large sauté pan over medium heat for 3 minutes. Add the olive oil and the onion. Cook until the onion softens, about 2 minutes, stirring once or twice. Add the garlic and cook for 1 minute. Add the rice and toast for 30 seconds. Add the bay leaf and wine and bring to a simmer. Allow the wine to evaporate for 1 minute and then add the squid ink, stirring to coat the rice. Season with 1 teaspoon salt.

Add 1 cup of the warm fish stock to the rice. Cook in the fashion of risotto, stirring regularly, to allow the starch in the rice to thicken the dish (the ink acts as a thickener as well). Once most of the stock has been absorbed, about 5 minutes, add another 1 cup of stock, continuing to stir regularly.

Add the remaining ½ cup stock to the rice. Once the last addition of stock is absorbed, after 3 to 5 minutes, the rice should be cooked, but not mushy. Taste the rice. If it's too crunchy (the center of the grain is still raw), add up to ½ cup warm water. Also add additional salt now, if needed. Remove from the heat and stir in the lemon juice.

Serves 4

2	cups Fish Stock (opposite)
	Sea salt
1½	tablespoons olive oil
1	yellow onion, cut into medium dice
1	clove garlic, minced
1	cup Calasparra, Bomba, or Arborio rice
1	bay leaf
½	cup dry white wine
2	tablespoons squid or cuttlefish ink (available from many fishmongers)
	Juice of ½ lemon

CARROT STOCK

To make the stock, combine all of the ingredients in a stockpot. Bring to a boil over high heat, reduce the heat to medium-low, and simmer for 40 minutes. Strain the stock and use immediately, or let cool completely and store in an airtight container in the refrigerator for up to 3 days.

Makes 4 cups

- 2 large carrots, peeled and shredded (about 2 cups)
- 3 cloves garlic
- ½ fennel bulb, cut into large dice
- 1 small bunch fresh thyme
- 1 bay leaf
- 1 teaspoon black peppercorns
- ½ teaspoon fennel seeds
- 4 cups water

FISH STOCK

Combine all the ingredients in a stockpot and bring to a simmer over medium heat. Skim the foam that forms on the top of the stock and reduce the heat to low to maintain a bare simmer. Simmer for 30 minutes, skimming the foam off periodically. Remove from the heat and pour through a fine-mesh strainer. Cool the stock and store, refrigerated in an airtight container, for up to 4 days (or frozen for several months).

Makes 4 cups

- 4 cups water
- 1 cup white wine
- 1 pound fish bones, from mild white-fleshed fish such as cod, hake, or halibut
- 1 medium yellow onion, peeled and quartered
- 4 cloves garlic
- 1 bulb fennel, quarted
- 2 stalks celery, cut into 4-inch lengths
- 1 leek, split in half lengthwise and rinsed (optional)
- 1 handful parsley stems (save leaves for another use)
- 1 tablespoon black peppercorns
- 1 fresh bay leaf

MUSHROOM STOCK

In a stockpot, combine all of the ingredients. Bring to a boil over high heat, then reduce the heat to medium-low and simmer for 1 hour. Strain the stock and use immediately, or let cool completely and store in an airtight container in the refrigerator for up to 3 days.

Makes 4 cups

- 2 cups mushroom stems
- ¼ ounce dried mushrooms (any variety)
- 1 leek, white and tender green parts only, split lengthwise and rinsed
- 5 cloves garlic
- ½ bulb fennel, cut into large dice
- 1 small bunch fresh thyme
- 1 bay leaf
- 1 teaspoon black peppercorns
- ½ teaspoon coriander seeds
- 4 cups water

AGED IN SOLERA SYSTEM

FLOR IS THAT GOOD YEAST

Sanlúcar de Barrameda

Jerez de la Frontera

El Puerto de Santa María

PRODUCED in the SHERRY TRIANGLE

FINO
Huertas

JEREZ XÉRÈS SHERRY

H·0701

FINO   AMONTILLADO OLOROSO

FiDEOS CON CHORIZO Y ALMEJAS

ANGEL HAIR WITH CHORIZO AND CLAMS

In Italy, there are endless shapes and varieties of pasta; in Spain, traditionally there's only one: *fideos*. These thin, angel hair–like noodles have long been added to soups, and somewhere along the line, Spaniards starting to cook them in the manner of paella. As is so often the case, there are many tales of how this recipe developed, but my favorite involves a fishing crew whose captain was a glutton for rice, so the crew began to cook fideos in the manner of rice to deter him from eating more than his fair share.

In many ways, fideos is easier to make than paella—it's certainly faster, and you don't have to worry about developing the *soccorat*, the crispy crust on the bottom of the paella pan. Accordingly, unlike paella, you can stir during cooking, making it easier to cook evenly without a massive pan and burner.

Preheat the oven to 350°F.

Break the pasta into 3-inch lengths (you can break about 12 strands at a time, and you should get 3 or 4 pieces from each strand). Spread the pasta out evenly on a baking sheet lined with parchment paper and bake for 4 to 6 minutes, until the pasta is toasted and has turned a deep golden brown. Remove from the oven and set aside.

In a medium paella pan (10 or 12 inches) or a shallow ovenproof sauté pan about the same size, combine the olive oil and chorizo over medium-high heat. Using a wooden spoon, break up the chorizo as it browns. (If you are using a firmer or precooked chorizo, you can just cut the chorizo into slices and brown those lightly.) When the chorizo is browned, reduce the heat to medium, add the onion and garlic, and sweat until the translucent, about 8 minutes.

While the vegetables are cooking, in a saucepan, bring the stock to a simmer, then remove from the heat. Season the stock with salt; start with 1 teaspoon. The fideos will be flavored and seasoned by absorbing the stock, so it's important that the stock is seasoned but not overseasoned, making the noodles salty. If your stock tastes salty at any point while you're seasoning it, just add some water.

recipe continues

Serves 4 (or 2 as a main dish)

½	pound angel hair or vermicelli pasta (we like De Cecco brand)
2	tablespoons olive oil
¼	pound fresh chorizo
1	yellow onion, cut into small dice
3	cloves garlic, minced
3½	cups chicken stock
	Salt
½	cup amontillado, fino, or manzanilla sherry
12	clams (small varieties like cockles, Manilas, or littlenecks all work well), scrubbed and purged (see page 38)
¼	cup dry white wine
1	cup English peas, fresh or frozen
1	tablespoon chopped fresh flat-leaf parsley
1	teaspoon fresh lemon juice
2	tablespoons Aïoli (page 80)

Add the toasted pasta to the pan with the vegetables and stir to coat with the fat in the pan. Raise the heat to high and add the sherry. Simmer to cook out the alcohol, about 2 minutes, and then add about one-third of the warm chicken stock. When the stock is nearly absorbed, give the pan a stir and add another one-third of the stock and return to a simmer.

Meanwhile, in a sauté pan or pot with a tight-fitting lid, bring the wine to a boil over high heat. Add the clams, discarding any that are open and do not close to the touch. Cover and cook until the clams open. This should take between 2 and 6 minutes, depending on the variety of clams. Be sure not to let them cook much longer after they have opened, because they'll get tough. Remove from the heat and discard any clams that failed to open. Dump the clams into a colander lined with cheesecloth and placed over a bowl to capture the broth. Set the clams and broth aside.

Preheat the broiler to high and position the rack about 2 inches from the heat source.

When the second addition of stock has been absorbed by the pasta, add the remaining chicken stock. Give it a stir to make sure none of the noodles are sitting above the stock. When most of the stock has been absorbed, stir in the peas, parsley, lemon juice, and reserved clam broth. Simmer until there is only ¼ to ½ inch of liquid in the bottom of the pan. If you have a cazuela or earthenware dish that can withstand high heat, transfer the fideos into that dish; otherwise you can finish and serve the dish in the same pan you're cooking it in.

Arrange the clams in their shells around the circumference of the pan, tilting them forward so that the bottom shell is dug into the noodles a bit and the clam meat will be protected from the high heat of the broiler. Place the entire pan under the broiler and toast for about 1 minute, until the top gets a bit crispy. (This top crust is much like the crispy soccarat at the bottom of paella, but in reverse—and easier to monitor.)

Like so many of our dishes, we like to serve this with the Aïoli right over the top.

CARNE

MOST TRADITIONAL Spanish meat and poultry dishes fall into one of two categories: roasts or stews. In the colder months, our approach to many of the meat and fish dishes remains relatively traditional; but during the warmer months, we've found ways to lighten the fare and make it appealing—even on the hottest of days. For example, we reworked classic stews such as Pato a la Sevillana and Cordero al Chilindrón as pan-roasted breast and chops, respectively, with sauces inspired by the originals.

Perhaps the signature meat specialty of Spain is cured pork. Jamón, the salted and dried leg, reigns supreme, but countless other pork charcuterie items are available and beloved—so much so that in Madrid there is a chain of restaurants called Museo de Jamón. We prepare a handful of different pork sausages (including a Basque-inspired hot dog) in addition to the Spanish cured pork items that we offer.

PATO A LA SEVILLANA

DUCK BREAST WITH SHERRY SAUCE

This is a perfect example of a common approach of ours—discovering an old-school recipe in a dated Spanish cookbook and using that to create something new. Historically, *pato a la sevillana* is a heavy braised stew. We use many of the same components to build an intense sauce that complements the crispy-skinned, blushing medium-rare duck breast.

We like to serve the sautéed Catalan greens used for stuffing the Piquillos Rellenos (page 25) alongside this duck.

To make the sauce, cut the onion, fennel, and carrot into large (about 1-inch) chunks. In a large pot over high heat, combine the olive oil, onion, fennel, carrot, and garlic. Cook for 3 minutes, stirring a few times to get deep, fast caramelization. Add the thyme, peppercorns, coriander, fennel seeds, and bay leaf. Cook for 1 minute, stirring constantly. Pour in the sherry and red wine and deglaze the pot, using a wooden spoon to scrape up any browned bits from the pan bottom. Bring to a simmer, reduce the heat to medium, and reduce the wines to about ½ cup. Add the stock, return to a simmer, and cook until reduced by half. Stir in the vinegar and season with salt. Remove from the heat, strain, discarding the solids, and cover to keep warm; you'll finish the sauce after the duck is cooked.

Season the duck breasts generously on both sides with salt and pepper. Choose a heavy-bottomed sauté pan large enough to hold the breasts without crowding. Place the pan over medium heat and add the olive oil. Arrange the duck breasts in the pan, skin-side down. Reduce the heat to medium-low. Note: You are not looking for any sizzle, or much of a reaction at all—the pan should be barely warm so that the duck fat has time to render out as the skin slowly crisps. Cook over medium-low heat for 15 minutes, periodically peeking at the skin to make sure it's browning evenly. After 15 minutes, the skin should be crispy and golden. Flip the breasts and add the thyme and garlic to the pan. Cook on the flesh side until slightly browned, about 3 more minutes. If you gently squeeze the sides of the duck you should meet some resistance, but the texture should not be firm. The internal temperature should read 130˚F to 135˚F and will carry over a few more degrees while it rests.

Transfer the duck to a plate to rest for about 8 minutes. Move to a cutting board and cut as you please—we like to slice across the width of the breast on a slight bias into slices about ½ inch thick.

When ready to serve, gently rewarm the sauce and stir in the butter and any juices that have collected on the plate that the duck was on. As the butter melts, add the olives, pearl onions, and Garlic Confit. Arrange the duck slices on 4 plates, spoon the sauce over, and serve immediately.

Serves 4

For the sauce:

1	red onion
1	fennel bulb
1	carrot, peeled
1	tablespoon olive oil
5	cloves garlic
5	sprigs fresh thyme
1	teaspoon black peppercorns
1	teaspoon ground coriander
1	teaspoon fennel seeds
1	bay leaf
2	cups amontillado sherry
¾	cup dry red wine
4	cups duck stock or chicken stock
4	tablespoons Pedro Ximénez sherry vinegar or other aged sherry vinegar
	Salt

2	boneless duck breasts, trimmed of excess fat and fat side lightly scored
	Salt and freshly ground black pepper
1	teaspoon olive oil
2	sprigs fresh thyme
2	cloves garlic, lightly crushed

1	tablespoon unsalted butter
20	manzanilla olives, pitted
12	Pickled Pearl Onions (page 45)
12	cloves Garlic Confit (page 18)

PoLLo AsAdo

ROAST CHICKEN WITH GUINDILLA PEPPER SAUCE

While simple roasted meats are a staple throughout Spain, our roast chicken is heavily influenced by the Italian *pollo alla diavalo*, a dish I prepared countless times as a sous chef in an Italian kitchen. The backbone of the sauce comes from spicy pickled pepper brine, but we also add Spanish cider (although any bone-dry cider will do) to reinforce the snappy tartness. You can roast the chicken in any manner you like, but again following an Italian lead, we borrow the idea of cooking chicken "under a brick."

The day before cooking, if possible, season the chicken pieces with salt, pepper, and half of the thyme leaves. Cover and refrigerate until ready to cook. If you can't season the chicken the day before, try to do so at least an hour before cooking.

To make the sauce, heat a large saucepan over medium heat. Add the 1 tablespoon olive oil, onion, garlic, and fennel. Sweat for 5 minutes, stirring occasionally. Season with salt. Add the bay leaf, thyme, pepper, and fennel seeds and toast, stirring, for 2 minutes. Add the cider, bring to a simmer, and cook until the liquid is reduced by half, about 3 minutes. Add the chicken stock and guindilla brine. Return the sauce to a simmer and cook until the liquid is reduced by half again, about 20 minutes longer. Add the sugar and stir to dissolve. Taste and adjust the seasoning. Remove from the heat and set aside. You could make this up to a few days beforehand, and refrigerate and reheat before serving.

When you're ready to cook the chicken, preheat the oven to 400°F. Heat a large cast-iron frying pan or heavy-bottomed sauté pan over medium heat for 3 minutes. Add the 2 tablespoons olive oil and the chicken pieces, skin-side down. With a sheet of aluminum foil placed in between, lay a heavy pot or pan on top of the chicken to create the "under a brick" effect.

Transfer to the oven and roast for 10 minutes. Remove the pan from the oven, remove the weight and foil from the chicken, and flip the pieces. Place the pan on the stovetop over medium-high heat and add the crushed garlic and the remaining thyme. Cook for 3 minutes, then transfer the breasts to a platter. Return the pan with the legs, thighs, and wings to the oven and roast until cooked through, 8 to 10 minutes longer. Remove from the oven and transfer the remaining chicken pieces to the platter. Discard any excess oil or fat in the pan, but leave in the garlic and thyme and place the pan over medium-high heat. Pour the sauce into the pan. Once again, cook to reduce the sauce by half, then reduce the heat to medium and add the butter, swirling the pan to incorporate the butter as it melts.

Ladle some sauce onto a large serving platter. Arrange the chicken in the pool of sauce. Top with the guindilla peppers and serve immediately with the remaining sauce on the side.

Serves 4

1	whole chicken, cut into 8 pieces (2 thighs, 2 legs, 2 wings, and 2 boneless breasts)
	Salt and freshly ground pepper
	Leaves from 4 sprigs fresh thyme

For the sauce:

1	tablespoon olive oil
1	Spanish onion, thinly sliced
5	cloves garlic, smashed
¼	fennel bulb, thinly sliced
	Salt
1	bay leaf
5	sprigs fresh thyme
2	teaspoons freshly ground black pepper
1	teaspoon fennel seeds
1	cup Spanish cider, such as Isastegi
4	cups chicken stock
1	cup guindilla pepper pickle brine (see page 17)
2	teaspoons sugar
2	tablespoons olive oil
4	cloves garlic, lightly crushed
2	tablespoons unsalted butter
8	pickled guindilla peppers

POLLO EN PEPITORIA

CHICKEN FRICASSEE

This is one of several dishes that I discovered paging through old Spanish cookbooks—from the likes of Penelope Casas, Simone Ortega, Paula Wolfert, and Miramar Torres—and of which I have never eaten a version except my own. What attracted me to the dish was that it utilizes some of Spain's greatest ingredients—saffron, almonds, and jamón—to elevate humble chicken. We tweaked the classic version a bit, removing the egg from the sauce and instead using hard-boiled eggs, peas, and parsley to make a little salad to brighten the stewed chicken.

Preheat the oven to 350°F.

Season the chicken with salt and pepper. Dredge the chicken in the flour to lightly coat on all sides.

Place a large Dutch oven or other heavy ovenproof pot over medium heat and add 1 tablespoon of the olive oil and 1 tablespoon of the butter. Add the chicken, skin-side down, and sear until nicely browned, 4 to 5 minutes. Flip and brown the second side for about 3 minutes. Transfer the chicken to a large plate.

Melt the remaining 1 tablespoon butter in the remaining 1 tablespoon olive oil in the pot over medium heat. Add the onions, garlic, and jamón. Sauté until the onions soften, about 5 minutes, stirring occasionally. Add the thyme, bay leaf, and saffron and season with salt and pepper. Cook for 1 more minute to allow the flavors of the spices to toast and intensify. Pour in the wine and deglaze the pan, using a wooden spoon to scrape up any browned bits on the bottom of the pan.

Return the chicken to the pot and add the crushed tomatoes with their juices and the chicken stock. If the liquid doesn't cover the chicken, add a little more stock or water as needed. Taste the broth and add salt, if needed. Bring to a simmer, then cover the pot and transfer to the oven.

Braise for 45 minutes. Remove the pot from the oven and carefully test the meat for doneness; it should pull away from the bone easily, but not fall apart. If the meat is still tightly clinging to the bones, return to the oven for 5 to 10 more minutes. Using a ladle, transfer about 1 cup of the braising liquid to a blender. Add the almonds and vinegar and blend until smooth. Stir the almond purée back into the pot to thicken the sauce.

To compose the salad, add the diced eggs, peas, and parsley to a bowl, and dress with the olive oil and lemon juice. Season with salt and pepper.

To serve, spoon 2 pieces of chicken and a ladleful of sauce into each of four plates or into shallow bowls and top each with a couple spoonfuls of the salad.

Serves 4

1	whole chicken, cut into 8 pieces
	Salt and freshly ground black pepper
1	cup all-purpose flour
2	tablespoons olive oil
2	tablespoons unsalted butter
2	Spanish onions, cut into medium dice
3	cloves garlic, thinly sliced
½	cup diced jamón
1	tablespoon chopped fresh thyme
1	bay leaf
1	pinch saffron threads
1	cup dry white wine
1½	cups canned crushed tomatoes, with juices
3	cups chicken stock, or more if needed
⅓	cup Marcona almonds
1	tablespoon plus 1 teaspoon Chardonnay vinegar or white wine vinegar

For the salad:

2	hard-boiled eggs, diced (see page 21)
1	cup English peas, fresh or frozen, blanched (see page 72)
1	cup loosely packed fresh flat-leaf parsley leaves
2	teaspoons olive oil
1	teaspoon fresh lemon juice
	Salt and freshly ground black pepper

CODORNIZ AL VERMUT

QUAIL WITH VERMOUTH GLAZE

Just as creative bartenders look to the kitchen for inspiration, at the restaurant I look to the bar; we often cook with our house vermouth, which allows us to create a dish that is uniquely ours. Quail are common in Spain, and while they may not be easy to find here, they are easy to cook and worth seeking out. Particularly when butterflied (as they are often sold), the birds cook in a manner of minutes—and quail is forgiving, in that it eats well whether it is cooked medium or well done.

Arroz con Champiñones (page 109) and Batatas con Mojo Picón (page 84) make nice accompaniments for the quail.

To make the glaze, in a small saucepan, combine the vermouth and sugar. Bring to a simmer, stirring to help dissolve the sugar. Cook until reduced by half, about 10 minutes. Stir in the vinegar. Remove from the heat and set aside.

Preheat the oven to 400°F.

Season the quail on both sides with salt and pepper.

Heat a large ovenproof sauté pan over medium-high heat. Add the olive oil and quail, skin-side (breast-side) down. Sear for 2 minutes, then add the garlic cloves and thyme springs, tucking them around the birds. Cook for about 2 minutes longer; the skin should be lightly golden. Flip the quail and spoon or brush with half of the glaze. Transfer to the oven and roast until the breasts are firm to the touch, about 5 minutes longer. Remove from the oven and spoon the remaining glaze over the quail. Tent loosely with aluminum foil and let rest for 5 minutes, then serve.

Serves 4

For the vermouth glaze:

1 cup Red Vermouth (page 203) or Carpano Antica Formula vermouth

3 tablespoons sugar

1 teaspoon red wine vinegar

4 whole quail, butterflied (breast- and backbones removed)

Salt and freshly ground black pepper

1 tablespoon olive oil

4 cloves garlic, lightly crushed

4 sprigs fresh thyme

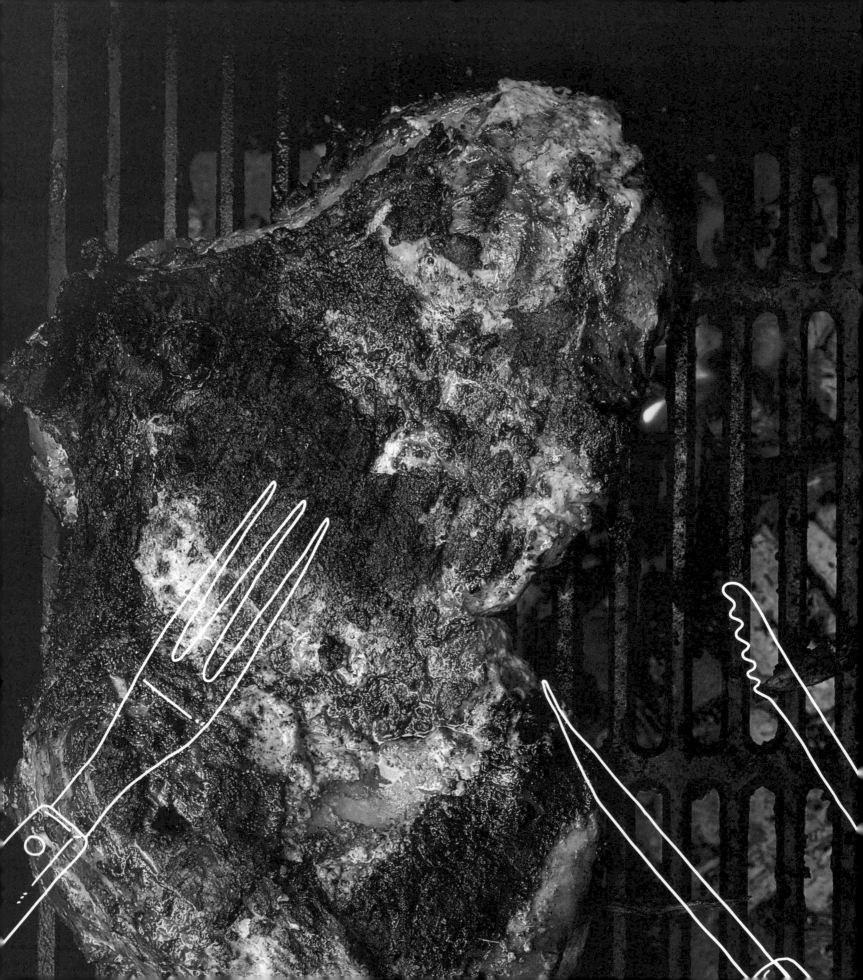

CORDERO A LA PARRILLA

GRILLED LEG OF LAMB

Whether you're on a vineyard in the Catalan countryside or in a Brooklyn backyard, there's something magical about cooking outdoors. Growing up in the city, I found grilling elusive. My first opportunities came in Maine, where my family spent a few weeks each summer. I insisted that we buy a pint-sized Weber grill (and then two).

As of this year, for the first time in my life, I have a bit of outdoor space in the city and, accordingly, my first grill. Leg of lamb is one of my favorite foods to grill for a group. Lamb feels luxurious—a treat for guests—but the leg is an economical cut. It's also handy that a butterflied leg varies in thickness—meaning you'll end up with some portions that are rare and some medium-rare, as well as some corners and flaps that make it close to well-done, so everyone is bound to find a few slices that are cooked just to their liking.

While grilled lamb in very traditional in Spain, and regularly part of a *calçotada* (see page 91), our recipe, which uses a yogurt marinade, can't be categorized as authentic. But we're fine with that! And as part of a calçotada feast or otherwise, Romesco Sauce (page 143) makes a great sauce for the lamb; but you could simply hit it with a bit of olive oil and lemon juice before serving. Potatoes, roasted simply with a bit of rosemary, or some grilled peppers, would be fantastic alongside.

Note that for the best results, you should start marinating the lamb the day before cooking.

The day before grilling, marinate the lamb: In a dry frying pan over medium heat, toast the fennel seeds, coriander seeds, and black peppercorns, stirring a few times, until fragrant, 2 or 3 minutes. Transfer the toasted spices to a food processor and add the garlic, rosemary, red pepper flakes, and olive oil. Process until a rough paste forms, scraping down the sides of the work bowl if necessary. Add the salt, fennel fronds, and yogurt and process until smooth.

Put the lamb in a large baking dish or on a large rimmed baking sheet. Massage the yogurt marinade into the lamb on all sides. Cover and refrigerate for at least 12 hours and up to 24 hours.

When you're ready to cook, remove the lamb from the fridge to take the chill off while you build a hot fire in a charcoal grill. Light your coals (preferably with a chimney starter or other means of avoiding lighter fluid)—if you're not grilling over charcoal, it's almost not worth bothering.

Once the coals are hot, spread them out evenly to create a uniformly hot, but not inferno-hot, cooking area. Remove the lamb from the marinade, wiping off the excess. Arrange the lamb on the grill rack. While some chefs might recommend not "messing with your meat" too much, and only flipping it once, I recommend flipping it every few minutes. This allows the meat to cook more evenly, and also helps prevent sections of the surface from burning, as they have a chance to cool down when they aren't facing the coals. The cooking time will vary widely based on how hot your grill is and how thick your lamb is, but somewhere between 15 and 25 minutes should do the trick. For medium-rare, the thickest part of the leg should register around 135°F on an instant-read thermometer, or use the thumb test (see page 143).

Transfer the meat to a platter, and let rest for a good 10 minutes to allow the juices to redistribute. Carve into thin slices against the grain on a bias and serve.

Serves 10 to 12

1	teaspoon fennel seeds
1	teaspoon coriander seeds
1	teaspoon black peppercorns
3	cloves garlic
1	tablespoon fresh rosemary leaves
½	teaspoon red pepper flakes
2	tablespoons olive oil
3	tablespoons salt
2	tablespoons fennel fronds
2	cups full-fat Greek yogurt
1	leg of lamb (6 to 8 pounds), butterflied

CORDERO AL CHILINDRÓN

LAMB CHOPS WITH ÑORA PEPPER PASTE

As with the Pato a la Sevillana (page 124), in our take on *cordero al chilindrón*, we transform a typical regional hearty stew into a summertime hit—or, simply something to be enjoyed with a half-dozen other dishes, rather than in its traditional role as a gut-busting solo attraction. Historically a saucy braise using tougher cuts like shank or shoulder and highlighting Spanish dried peppers, in this version of chilindrón, we make an intense dried Ñora pepper paste to serve with simply cooked chops, loin, or saddle.

To make the pepper paste, put the peppers in a heatproof bowl and cover them with 1½ cups boiling water. Place a small dish on top of the peppers to prevent them from floating and rehydrate for at least 20 minutes. Drain the peppers, reserving ½ cup of the steeping liquid. Using your hands, pull the peppers open and discard the seeds and stems.

Place the cleaned Ñora peppers, the piquillo peppers, garlic, vinegar, and steeping liquid in a blender and process on high speed. Turn the speed down to medium and in the olive oil until a smooth paste forms. Season with salt and set aside.

Season the lamb chops with salt and pepper on both sides. Heat a large cast-iron or other heavy-bottomed sauté pan over medium-high heat for 2 to 3 minutes. Add the olive oil to the hot pan and then the chops. Cook for 2 minutes, and then add the garlic cloves and rosemary sprigs, tucking them around the pan. Cook for 1 more minute, then flip the chops and cook for 2 minutes on the second side. For medium-rare, an instant-read thermometer inserted into the thickest part of a chop should register 130°F, or use the thumb test (see page 143). Transfer the lamb to a plate, and let rest for 5 minutes.

Discard the garlic and rosemary from the pan but keep it over medium-high heat and add the piquillo peppers. Char on one side until deeply caramelized, about 3 minutes. Flip the peppers and deglaze the pan with the sherry, using a wooden spoon to scrape up any browned bits from the pan bottom. Season the peppers with salt and pepper and let the sherry reduce until almost entirely evaporated, but just a little bit of moisture remains in the pan.

To serve, using a pastry brush, paint a streak of the pepper paste across the bottom of each plate (or use a spoon). Arrange 3 lamb chops and two charred piquillo peppers on each plate, alternating and overlapping them like shingles, partially on top of the pepper paste. Garnish with the fennel fronds and a drizzle of olive oil. We like to finish our meats with a sprinkle of coarse Maldon salt. Serve immediately.

Serves 4

For the pepper paste:

- 5 Ñora peppers (you can substitute 3 ancho chiles)
- 2 piquillo peppers
- ½ clove garlic
- 1 tablespoon Pedro Ximénez sherry vinegar or other aged sherry vinegar
- 1 tablespoon olive oil
- Salt

- 12 baby lamb chops, about 2 ounces each
- Salt and freshly ground black pepper
- 2 tablespoons olive oil
- 3 cloves garlic, lightly crushed
- 2 sprigs fresh rosemary
- 8 piquillo peppers
- ½ cup amontillado sherry
- ½ cup fennel fronds or fresh parsley sprigs
- Sea salt, such as Maldon, for garnish

Chuleta de Puerco con Piperrada Picante

Pork Chops with Peppers

A sauce so nice, we've included it twice. Piperrada, like romesco, is one of the Spanish sauces that has made it beyond Spanish restaurants and can be frequently found in all sorts of places. To complement pork chops, which at their best have a healthy layer of fat, in this variation of our piperrada, we added some extra heat and acid in the form of pickled cherry peppers and a splash of their brine. Fresh oregano replaces the thyme for its more assertive flavor.

A glass of dry cider would be just right here.

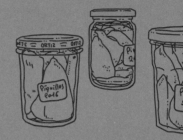

To make the piperrada, refer to the Migas con Piperrada recipe on page 65, making the following adjustments:

- Replace the chopped thyme with the oregano.

- When you add the roasted, peeled, and sliced peppers to the sautéed onions, also add the chopped cherry peppers and use the pickled pepper brine in place of the sherry vinegar.

- Omit the bacon and tomatoes from the pipperrada, though you could chose to keep them in.

Season the pork chops with salt and pepper on both sides. Heat a cast-iron or other heavy-bottomed sauté pan over medium-high heat for 2 minutes. Add the olive oil to the hot pan and then the chops. Cook until deeply caramelized on the first side, 4 to 5 minutes. Flip the chops and add the butter, swirling the pan to help it melt. Add the garlic cloves and thyme sprigs, tucking them around the pan.

Raise the heat to high. When the butter foams, baste the pork by tilting the pan towards you so that the butter pools and rapidly, repeatedly spooning the foaming butter all over the chops. Cook for 4 to 5 minutes longer. The chops are done when an instant-read thermometer inserted into the thickest part of a chop registers 145°F to 150°F, or use the thumb test (testing for a medium cook, see page 143); they should be warm, but not hot, in the center. Transfer the chops to a plate, tent with aluminum foil, and let rest for 5 minutes.

To serve, slice the chops or dish them up whole. Pile the piperrada on top and serve immediately.

Serves 4

For the Piperrada Sauce:

2	red bell peppers
1	yellow bell pepper
1	green bell pepper (optional)
3	tablespoons olive oil
	Salt and freshly ground black pepper
1	yellow onion, thinly sliced
3	cloves garlic, sliced
1	teaspoon chopped fresh oregano
½	cup dry white wine
¼	cup chopped pickled cherry peppers
½	cup pickled cherry pepper brine

4	pork chops, about 1 inch thick
	Salt and freshly ground black pepper
1	tablespoon olive oil
2	tablespoons unsalted butter
2	cloves garlic, lightly crushed
5	sprigs fresh thyme

Asturian Cider House

ASADILLO
83

TORTILLA ESPAÑOLA
52

POLLO ASADO
127

FABADA
141

FLAN
182

BEVERAGE PAIRING

SIDRA

In Asturias, in north-central Spain, apples are everywhere and the *sidra,* or cider, is free-flowing. So much so, that with the flair of a bullfighter, local servers pour cider with an arm extended towards the sky, the other holding a thin glass as low as possible, their backs turned from the table, the cider falling a few fantastic feet before splashing both into the glass and all over the floor. This serves a function as well, aerating the astringent apple brew and thus making it a bit easier to enjoy. It is that sharp tartness, as well as natural fermentation funk, that makes sidra an ideal pairing for the rich hearty stews and roasts of the region.

Furthermore, Americans are increasingly open to and excited about those flavor profiles: funky and sour (and bitter) as opposed to sweet or balanced, making sidra an exciting revelation for many of our guests. Our cider house menu features straightforward roast chicken as well as perhaps the most iconic dish of the region— *fabada* (page 141), a rendition of pork and beans not dissimilar from the cassoulet of nearby southern France.

BACON

BLOOD SAUSAGE

CHORIZO

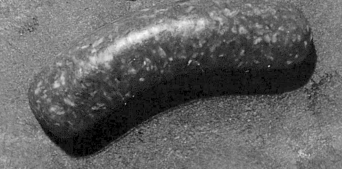

FABADA ASTURIANA

ASTURIAN PORK AND BEANS

Pork and beans are friends. Ask anyone. In Asturias, north-central Spain, this duo is the pride of the people (along with the local cider)—you even find "kits" for making this regional specialty at nearly every stall in the local markets, which include dried beans, *morcilla* (blood sausage), chorizo, and pork belly. Our version is relatively traditional, but instead of cooking the meats with the beans, we cook the beans with a *jamón* bone and then sear the bacon and sausages and serve them on top; that way we can be sure the meats don't overcook. A smoked ham hock can be substituted for the jamón bones, and will add a pleasant smoky quality to the beans.

The night before preparing the fabada, pick over the beans for any stones or grit. Put in a large bowl, add the water, and refrigerate overnight.

The next day, drain the beans. Place in a pot, add enough water to cover by 2 inches, and bring to a bare simmer over medium-low heat.

Meanwhile, peel the onion, keeping the root end attached, and cut in half top-to-bottom so that the root end keeps the halves intact. Wash the carrot and cut in half lengthwise. Rinse the head of garlic and cut in half side-to-side so that it remains intact.

Add the onion, carrot, garlic, bay leaves, jamón bone, ½ cup of the olive oil, and the pimentón to the pot with the beans. Simmer the beans for 1 to 3 hours. (The cooking time for beans varies widely, but cooking them slowly, and therefore gently, helps ensure that they won't fall apart before they are perfectly tender.) When the beans are tender and no longer chalky inside, but the skins have not split, remove them from the heat, season with salt (you'll need a few tablespoons), and let cool at room temperature. (The beans can be covered and refrigerated for up to 3 days; reheat gently before serving.)

Preheat the oven to 400°F.

Place a large ovenproof sauté pan over medium heat. Add the bacon and cook until the fat is rendered and the bacon is slightly crispy, about 5 minutes. Transfer the bacon to a plate, reserving the fat in the pan. Add the chorizo and morcilla. Sear on the first side for 3 minutes, then flip and transfer to the oven. Roast until both the chorizo and morcilla are warm in the center, about 6 minutes longer. Remove from the oven and transfer to a cutting board to rest for a few minutes. Slice the sausages.

To serve, spoon the warm beans into individual bowls or a serving dish and top with the bacon and slices of sausage. Serve immediately.

Serves 4

2	cups dried fabe, emergo, corona, fava or other large bean
5	cups water
1	Spanish onion
1	head garlic
1	carrot
2	bay leaves
1	jamón bone or smoked ham hock
1	tablespoon sweet pimentón
	Salt
½	cup olive oil
2	links fresh chorizo
2	links precooked morcilla (blood sausage) (optional)
4	ounces slab bacon, diced
1	tablespoon Pedro Ximénez sherry vinegar or other aged sherry vinegar

BISTEC CON ROMESCO

FLAT-IRON STEAKS WITH ROMESCO SAUCE

For a chef, it can be tempting to serve creative dishes to impress your guests, but a dish that "hits the spot" is often much more pleasing than one that surprises. You can use any cut of beef that you'd like, but we like flat-iron because it is both flavorful and economical. And if not steak, practically anything you grill can be happily topped with romesco.

While part of its inherent beauty is that it's complementary to any number of foods, the romesco sauce can be tweaked infinitely. You can process the sauce to varying degrees of smoothness to achieve different textures; or substitute a different type of nut (hazelnuts are also traditional); or remove the pimentón and add a dried chili pepper; or omit the piquillos and add roasted green bell peppers and parsley to make a *romesco verde*. It's just the sort of versatile base recipe that is handy to have in your repertoire.

Preheat the oven to 400°F. Line a baking sheet with parchment paper or aluminum foil.

Clean the spring onions, removing the green tops (save for another use) and root ends. Cut the onions lengthwise into quarters. In a bowl, toss the onions with 1 tablespoon of the olive oil, 3 sprigs of the thyme, and salt and pepper to taste. Transfer to the prepared baking sheet and spread in a single layer. Break up 2 tablespoons of the butter into 4 or 5 pieces and scatter on top. Sprinkle with the water. Place in the oven and roast until the onions are tender and browned in some places, about 20 minutes.

While the onions are roasting, season the steaks generously with salt and pepper on both sides. Place a cast-iron or other heavy-bottomed sauté pan over high heat. Heat for about 3 minutes, until almost smoking. Add the remaining 1 tablespoon olive oil to the hot pan and arrange the steaks in the oil. Sear on the first side for 4 minutes. (Naturally, steaks will vary in thickness, so adjust your timing as needed, but this is a good benchmark for a 1½-inch-thick steak.) Flip the steaks and add the garlic cloves and remaining 3 thyme sprigs, tucking them around the pan. Add the remaining 2 tablespoons butter and allow to melt and begin to foam. Baste your steaks by tilting your pan towards you so that the butter pools, then spooning the foaming butter over the steaks. Continue basting for about 1 minute.

The steaks are done when an instant-read thermometer inserted into the thickest part registers 135°F to 140°F for medium-rare, or use the thumb test (see opposite). (If your steak is thicker than 1½ inches, or if you would like it cooked further than medium-rare, you may need to place it into a 400°F oven for 3 to 5 minutes.) Transfer to a cutting board, and let rest for about 5 minutes. Carve across the grain on a bias into slices about ½ inch thick.

To serve, place the roasted spring onions on the bottom of a serving dish. Slice the steak and arrange the slices over the onions, overlapping them like shingles. Top with the romesco and serve immediately.

Serves 4

8	spring onions or shallots
2	tablespoons olive oil
6	sprigs fresh thyme
	Salt and freshly ground black pepper
4	tablespoons unsalted butter
2	tablespoons water
4	flat-iron steaks (or any cut), each about 6 ounces and 1½ inches thick
3	cloves garlic, lightly crushed
	Romesco Sauce (opposite), processed until coarse, for serving

ROMESCO SAUCE

Romesco, a descendent of a Roman sauce made with ground bread and nuts, can be left chunky or processed until smooth. Chunky, it makes a great condiment for a steak, but for dipping (as in this recipe), it's best to purée until smooth and homogenous. In a food processor, combine the almonds, croutons, and garlic and pulse until a more or less uniformly coarse (pea-sized) mixture forms. Add the peppers, olive oil, vinegar, pimento, salt, and water and process until smooth.

For a coarse romesco: Pulse just until a chunky, pestolike sauce comes together—perfect with fish, beef, lamb, and poultry.

Store any leftover sauce in an airtight container in the refrigerator for up to 1 week.

Makes 2 cups

- ¼ cup Marcona almonds
- ¼ cup toasted croutons
- 1 small clove garlic, chopped
- 1 cup stemmed piquillo peppers
- ½ cup olive oil
- 2 tablespoons sherry vinegar
- 1 teaspoon sweet pimentón
- 1 teaspoon salt
- ¼ cup water

THE THUMB TEST, AND LET IT REST

USING touch instead of a thermometer to determine doneness of meat is a very useful skill to acquire. Press the cooked steak or chop gently. For medium-rare, it should feel the same as touching the flesh under your thumb when you are touching your thumb and middle finger together. Likewise, rare meat will feel like touching your thumb to your index finger; medium-well is thumb to ring finger; and thumb-to-pinky tells you when it's well-done.

ALSO, for juicy, succulent results, it is crucial to let meat rest after cooking to allow the juices to redistribute throughout. A good rule of thumb is letting it rest for half as long as you cooked it. So if your steak took 8 minutes to cook, rest for it for 4 minutes.

"THE BASQUE DOG"

CHISTORRA SAUSAGE WITH PIQUILLO MOSTARDA AND AÏOLI

Making sausage is one of my favorite things to do. I find the transformation of a few rough hunks of meat and fat into an intensely flavorful yet balanced "package" to be endlessly satisfying. There's no shortage of Spanish sausage styles to emulate—chorizo, *butifarra*, and *morcilla*, to name a few. But it is our *chistorra* that often steals the show. Chistorra is a Basque variety of sausage, similar in flavor to chorizo but ground more finely and packed into a lamb casing rather than pork; its size and texture resembles that of a classic American hot dog. So much so that we began to serve our chistorra on a potato roll—and that's how our Spanish hot dog was born.

Making sausage at home requires several pieces of equipment and a good deal of effort. Do not page past this recipe, though—you can buy good-quality hot dogs and serve them up with our fixings. This won't quite yield a Basque Dog, but it won't be bad either! If you can find chistorra sausage, you should certainly use that (Despaña in New York City makes their own, which you can order online), or you can use fresh chorizo and serve that on a bun with mostarda and aïoli, as below.

Cook the dogs as you like. You can grill them or boil them, but we like to fry them to get a snappy exterior.

Butter the cut sides of the potato rolls and toast them on a grill or under a broiler.

To build the Basque Dogs, spread Aïoli on one side of each bun, tuck a hot dog in each, and spoon the mostarda to taste over the top. No surprise: these are great with a cold beer . . . but try a Basque Dog with Basque cider or a kalimotxo (page 194), too!

Serves 4 to 8

8 chistorra or fresh chorizo sausages, or good-quality hot dogs (try to find pork-based hot dogs, but beef works)

2 tablespoons unsalted butter

8 potato rolls (we love Martin's)

Aïoli (page 80) for serving

Piquillo Mostarda (recipe follows) for serving

PIQUILLO MOSTARDA

To make the mostarda, in a large pot, combine the mustard seeds, mustard powder, sugar, salt, white wine vinegar, and sherry vinegar. Bring to a simmer, stirring to mix well. Cook until almost syrupy and reduced by half, about 30 minutes. Add the peppers, onion, garlic, and thyme. Return to a simmer and cook for about 30 minutes longer.

To check for doneness, spoon a bit of mostarda onto a chilled plate. When you run a finger through the mostarda, it should stay in place and hold its shape. If the mostarda is too loose, cook for another 15 to 20 minutes and test again—it should be thick and syrupy in the pot and hold its shape on the cold plate.

Let cool to room temperature, about 1 hour, and then if desired, stir just enough Dijon into the mostarda to give it a strong flavor (start with 1 tablespoon). Store the mostarda in an airtight container in the refrigerator for up to 1 month.

Makes 2 cups

1½ tablespoons mustard seeds

3 tablespoons dry mustard powder

¼ cup sugar

1 tablespoon salt

½ cup white wine vinegar

¼ cup sherry vinegar

1½ cups thinly sliced canned piquillo peppers

¼ cup thinly sliced red onion

2 cloves garlic, thinly sliced

1 teaspoon chopped fresh thyme

Dijon mustard (optional)

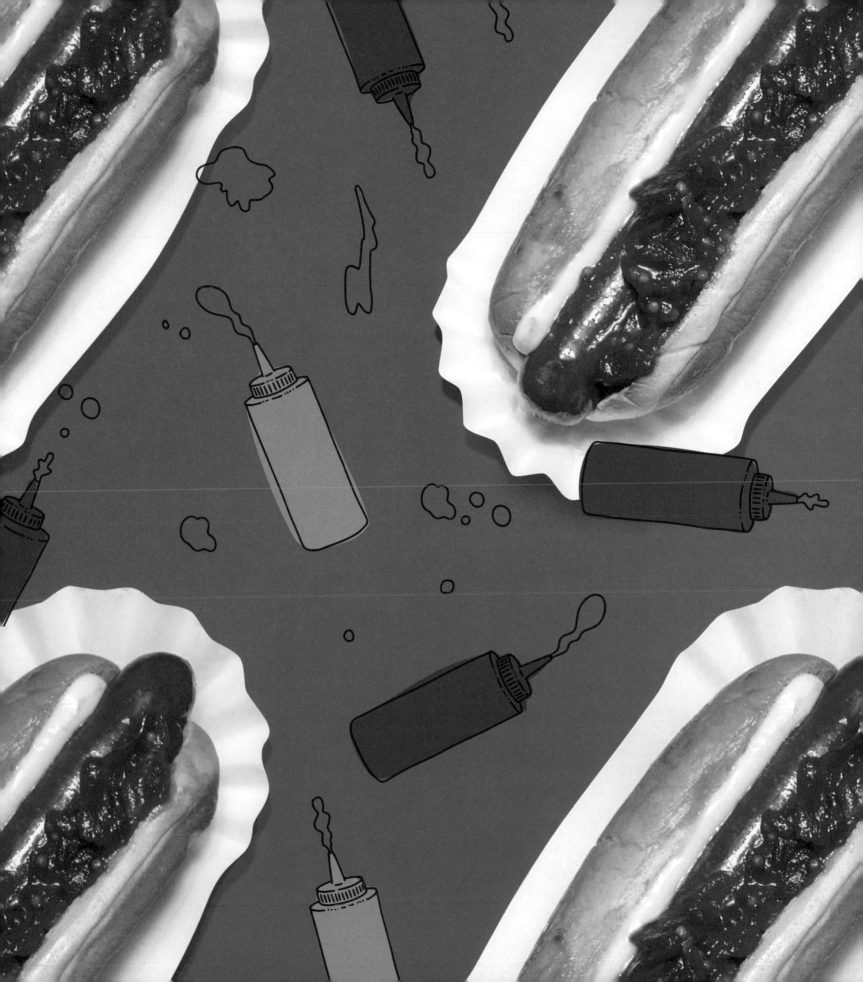

PESCADO

THE RESERVOIR OF ICONIC Spanish fish dishes is deep, and with so many classics to inspire us, our work has been to update vintage recipes to fit today's preferences. For instance, in the famed *pulpo a la gallega*, we don't serve the octopus straight from a pot of boiling water; we add an additional step of charring it before serving, which not only adds another layer of flavor, it appeals to Americans' desire for crunch. In our *salpicón*, we don't chop the seafood up into nearly unrecognizable pieces, choosing instead to leave the pieces larger so the diner can taste and appreciate each individual ingredient.

In some cases, we've simply been inspired by a dish's name and made it entirely our own, as with our spin on *zurrukatuna*, a traditional Basque fish dish whose name means, roughly, "tasty or inviting slurp"—the very sound of which inspired our summertime scallop dish, far from the original salt-cod stew.

GAMBAS AL AJILLO

GARLIC SHRIMP

Gambas al ajillo is one of the dishes that visitors to Spain seem to crave as soon as they get back home to the States. It's certainly one of the dishes that our guests come in asking for. Like *pan con tomate*, it's one of the traditional dishes that we love and prefer to serve unadulterated from the classic; but we serve it only when we can get the best-quality product. So, in this case, we offer the simple garlic-laced shrimp only when we can source fresh head-on shrimp.

Devein the shrimp (see Note), or have your fishmonger take care of this step for you. It's best to cook the shrimp in their shells, although at the restaurant we remove all but the tail and head before cooking to make the dish easier and less messy for our guests to eat.

Heat a large sauté pan over high heat for 2 minutes. (If your pan isn't large enough to fit all of the shrimp in a single layer without crowding, you will need to cook them in two batches or two pans.) Add the olive oil to the hot pan and then the garlic. Cook for 30 seconds, shaking the pan so the garlic toasts evenly.

Add the shrimp and cook for 90 seconds. Flip the shrimp and add the salt, red pepper flakes, and parsley. Cook, stirring, for 90 more seconds, then deglaze the pan with the wine, using a wooden spoon to scrape up any browned bits on the pan bottom. Cook for 1 minute longer.

Spoon into individual bowls or a serving bowl and serve immediately, with the lemon wedges and bread to soak up the garlicky oil.

NOTE: *To devein shrimp with the shell on, using small kitchen shears or a sharp paring knife (If the shrimp shells are already removed, it is easier to use a knife rather than a scissors), make an incision as shallow as possible along the curved back side of the shrimp to expose the vein (it will be a brownish-black color). Using the tip of your scissors or knife, or just your fingers, remove the vein.*

Serves 4

3 tablespoons olive oil

6 cloves garlic, thinly sliced

32 head-on jumbo (21/25 count) shrimp (about 1½ pounds), in their shells, deveined

2 teaspoons salt

½ teaspoon red pepper flakes

2 tablespoons chopped fresh flat-leaf parsley

½ cup dry white wine

1 lemon, cut into wedges

Crusty bread for serving

SALPICÓN

SEAFOOD SALAD WITH TOMATO-CLAM VINAIGRETTE

Salpicón translates roughly to "minced-up things"—which really doesn't mean much at all. For instance, one of the sauces for the Trucha a la Sal (page 172) is called salpicón as well. That said, quite frequently salpicón is a seafood salad with mixed chopped seafood tossed in vinaigrette. Inspired by that classic version of the dish, but looking to create a seafood salad that allows guests to enjoy the different flavors and textures of each ingredient without having them all mixed in each bite, we leave the ingredients larger so that each mouthful is distinct.

In a large pot with a tight-fitting lid, heat ½ cup of the olive oil over medium heat. Add the garlic and toast, stirring, for 2 minutes. Add the clams, discarding any that are open and do not close to the touch. Add the wine and parsley stems, if using. Cover tightly and steam for 3 minutes. Lift the lid every 30 seconds or so to see if the clams have opened; depending on the type of clams, they could all open in 3 minutes, or it may take up to an additional 5 minutes.

When all (or nearly all) the clams have opened, remove them from the heat and dump the contents of the pot into a colander placed over a bowl to catch the broth. Discard any clams that failed to open and set the clams aside to cool. Pour the broth through a fine-mesh strainer (lined with cheesecloth, if you have it) into a glass measuring jar to remove any sand or grit. Dilute the broth with half its volume of ice water and set aside.

When the clams are cool, shuck them into a bowl. Toss with 1 tablespoon of the olive oil and refrigerate until you are ready to serve. (You can prepare the clams and broth up to 1 day ahead of time.)

Place the peeled tomatoes in a blender with the diluted clam broth, the vinegar, the remaining 1 tablespoon olive oil, and salt. Blend until smooth. Set aside.

In a large bowl, combine the shucked clams, sliced octopus, poached shrimp, celery, fennel, onion, clam-tomato juice, and lemon juice. Stir well. Season with salt and pepper and more lemon juice, if needed. Spoon into individual bowls or a serving bowl. Top with the parsley, fennel fronds, chives, and celery leaves and serve immediately.

Serves 4

½   cup plus 2 tablespoons olive oil

2   cloves garlic, lightly crushed

2   pounds cockles (you can substitute Manila, littleneck, or other small clams), scrubbed and purged (see page 38)

½   cup dry white wine

1   handful fresh parsley stems (optional)

1   cup cherry tomatoes, peeled (see page 79)

1   tablespoon Chardonnay vinegar or other mild white vinegar

    Salt and freshly ground black pepper

1   Spanish octopus (1 to 2 pounds), pressure-cooked or braised in the oven as directed in Pulpo a la Gallega (page 154); omit the charring step and slice the tentacles into small rounds

12   poached shrimp, as directed in Ensalada de Huevos y Camarones (page 21)

2   celery stalks, peeled and thinly sliced

½   fennel bulb, thinly sliced

¼   red onion, thinly sliced

    Juice of ½ lemon

1   small handful each fresh flat-leaf parsley leaves, fennel fronds, chive batons (1-inch pieces), and the yellowish celery leaves that are attached to the core stalks (optional)

THIS DISH MAY SEEM SIMPLE BUT IT'S A PROVEN CROWD-PLEASER. IT HAILS FROM GALICIA, IN THE NORTHWEST OF SPAIN. GALICIA IS THE SEAFOOD CAPITAL OF SPAIN, AND AMONG THE TREMENDOUS VARIETY OF SEAFOOD DISHES FROM THAT REGION, *PULPO A LA FEIRA* (AS IT'S CALLED LOCALLY, WHICH TRANSLATES TO "FAIRGROUND OCTOPUS") IS THE KING. IT'S PRESENT AT EVERY FESTIVAL AND IS NOW WIDELY SERVED ALL OVER SPAIN. ITS POPULARITY AT FESTIVALS DATES BACK AS LONG AS THE FESTIVALS THEMSELVES, AND IT'S EASY TO SEE WHY. THE OCTOPUS IS INEXPENSIVE, LOCALLY AVAILABLE, AND CAN BE EASILY PREPARED IN LARGE QUANTITIES. FURTHERMORE, GALLEGANS CONTINUE TO DEBATE, JUST AS THE ANCIENT GREEKS DID, WHETHER OCTOPUS INCREASES MALE VIRILITY AND POTENCY—WHICH NO DOUBT ADDS SOME INTRIGUE TO THE PARTY!

OCTOPUS GALICIAN-STYLE WITH PIMENTÓN AND SEA SALT

My first encounter with *pulpo a la gallego* was at Macieras, a Gallegan restaurant in Madrid (see page 112). But several years later, I was able to sample the specialty in its native setting: market day in Padrón, Galicia (see more on this capital of peppers on page 86). It was there that I stood shoulder-to-shoulder with the locals while we all watched with anticipation as an octopus emerged from a giant cauldron, speared on a large fish hook. It was then snipped with shears onto wood plates called *cachelos*, topped with a few cubes of boiled potatoes, and doused with a generous pour of olive oil from a tin watering can. Everything was generously doused with sea salt and smoked paprika. Washed down with the local brew, Estrella Galicia, it made for a memorable breakfast.

The traditional method of preparation is simply to boil the local octopus, pretty much just as I saw on that day. The octopus has first either been tenderized by freezing or, historically, by pounding against a rock before simmering in a large copper pot, sometimes with a bit of onion and bay leaf. Our *pulpo* is certainly a close approximation of what you'd find in Spain, but we utilize a pressure cooker and add some char to the equation.

To cook the octopus in a pressure cooker: Rinse the octopuses thoroughly. Combine the octopus, olive oil, sherry, onion, garlic, thyme, bay leaf, and peppercorns in the cooker. Seal and cook on high pressure for 20 minutes.

To cook the octopus in the oven: Preheat the oven to 350°F. Rinse the octopuses thoroughly. In a large Dutch oven, combine the octopuses, olive oil, sherry, onion, garlic, thyme, bay leaf, peppercorns, and 2 cups water. Bring the ingredients to a simmer over high heat, then cover the pot with aluminum foil and then the lid and braise in the oven until tender, about 1½ hours.

Drain the octopus and let cool before cleaning. To clean, we like to use a pair of kitchen shears. Begin by cutting off the heads (discard or save for another use). Next cut the octopuses in half with 4 tentacles on each half. This will expose the beak just under the head. Remove the beak and cut between the tentacles, to make 8 pieces. (At this point you can store the octopus, in an airtight container in the refrigerator, for up to 3 days.)

To make the potatoes, follow the instructions in the first step of the Ensalada Russa recipe on page 20.

When you are ready to serve, heat a cast-iron or heavy-bottomed sauté pan over high heat until it's almost smoking and add just enough olive oil to cover the bottom. Add the octopus in a single layer, being careful not to overcrowd the pan (if your pan isn't big enough, cook in two batches or two pans). We like to put a grill weight over the octopus, but if you don't have one, place another pot or pan on top to press as much of each tentacle as possible into contact with the pan. Reduce the heat to medium-high and sear on the first side for 3 minutes (the tentacles should be pleasingly charred), then flip and cook on the second side for 2 more minutes.

While the octopus is cooking, arrange the potatoes on a serving dish. Using the bottom of a plate, smash the potatoes roughly. Pile the octopus over the potatoes and douse generously with olive oil. Sprinkle with sea salt, dust with pimentón, and serve immediately.

Serves 4

For the octopus:

2 Spanish octopuses, 1 to 2 pounds each

1 tablespoon olive oil

½ cup amontillado sherry

1 small yellow onion, quartered

3 cloves garlic

4 sprigs fresh thyme

1 bay leaf

10 black peppercorns

For the potatoes:

12 fingerling potatoes

2 tablespoons salt

1 bay leaf

5 sprigs fresh thyme

10 black peppercorns

Olive oil for searing and for drizzling

Maldon sea salt for sprinkling

Sweet pimentón for sprinkling

Bacalao al Pil Pil

COD WITH PIL PIL SAUCE

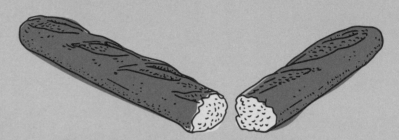

This is one of many classic Spanish, and particularly Basque, dishes that are in a large part about savoring the sauce, scooped up with bread, after the protein is gone. The dish is traditionally cooked in an earthenware dish called a *cazuela*, and *pil pil* is (theoretically) the sound that's created as you shake the dish against the stovetop. The reason for shaking is that the skin of the salt cod contains a lot of gelatin, and as it is stirred with the olive oil, the natural juices of the fish emulsify with the oil to form a creamy sauce. We don't use salt cod and also don't rely on shaking the pan to make the sauce work—we opt instead for a good blender.

Pour the fish stock into a blender. While the machine is running, slowly pour in ½ cup of the olive oil. Blend until smooth and emulsified. Add 1 teaspoon salt and process to blend well. Set the sauce aside.

Warm a large sauté pan over medium-high heat for 2 minutes. Add the remaining 2 tablespoons olive oil to the pan, then the garlic and the chile, if using. Let the garlic and chile toast for 30 seconds while you season the cod on both sides with salt.

Add the cod fillets to the pan and let cook, untouched, for 5 minutes. At this point, the fish should have taken on a bit of color and should willingly release from the pan to be flipped. Flip, add the sauce to the pan, and cook for 2 more minutes. Remove from the heat and stir in the chopped parsley and lemon juice.

Slide on individual plates and serve immediately, with bread for dipping.

Serves 4

- ½ cup Fish Stock (see page 115)
- ½ plus 2 tablespoons cup olive oil
- Sea salt
- 4 cloves garlic, lightly crushed
- 1 dried choricero (look in stores that carry imported Spanish products) or ancho chile (optional)
- 4 cod fillets, about 6 ounces each
- 2 tablespoons chopped fresh flat-leaf parsley
- Juice of ½ lemon
- Crusty bread for serving

RAPE A LA KOSKERA

MONKFISH WITH PEAS AND ALMONDS

Dishes that we created in previous years begin to creep back into our thoughts as the weather turns and our farmers' market visits gain a level of anticipation, wondering if this green or that fruit will be there. *Koskera*, a classic Basque fish preparation made with peas, almonds, and eggs, is one of our greenest dishes and a welcome departure from some of the less vibrant colors from our winter repertoire.

We seldom dust fish with flour, but Wondra, an ultra-fine flour, helps to develop a thin crust on a skinless piece of fish without becoming unpleasantly gummy.

To make the sauce, heat a sauté pan over medium-high heat. Add 1 tablespoon of the olive oil and the onion and garlic. Cook for about 5 minutes, until the onion to begins to brown and soften slightly. Add the almonds and toast with the onion for about 1 minute. Add the wine and simmer until it reduces by half. Remove from the heat and let cool slightly. Pour the contents of the pan into a blender. Add the blanched peas, pea stock, parsley, and fish stock (it's important that the stocks are cold). Blend on medium to high speed while slowly drizzling in the remaining ½ cup olive oil. Process until smooth and emulsified. Taste and add salt as needed. (The sauce can be made up to 1 day ahead of time, cooled, and stored, tightly covered, in the refrigerator.)

Season the fish medallions with salt and pepper and dust lightly with the flour. Heat a large sauté pan over medium-high for 2 minutes. Add 1 tablespoon of the olive oil to the hot pan and then lay the fish in the oil. (If the pan seems crowded, cook the fish in two batches or two pans.) Cook on the first side for 4 minutes. Flip and cook on the second side until the fish flakes when a fork is inserted, about 3 minutes longer. Remove from the heat and transfer the fish to a plate to rest.

While the fish is cooking, in a medium sauté pan or shallow pot, gently reheat the Koskera Sauce. When it is warm, but before it comes to a simmer (which will cause the sauce to break and become grainy), add the trio of blanched peas. Allow the peas to warm through, stirring for about 2 minutes, then remove from the heat and stir in the lemon juice. Taste and adjust the seasoning.

To serve, place 3 fish medallion on each of four individual plates or on a serving platter and spoon the sauce over. Sprinkle the chopped almonds over the top, followed by the peas shoots. Drizzle everything with the remaining 1 teaspoon olive oil and serve immediately.

Serves 4

For the Koskera Sauce:

- 1 tablespoon plus ½ cup olive oil
- 1 yellow onion, thinly sliced
- 2 cloves garlic, thinly sliced
- ½ cup Marcona almonds
- ⅓ cup dry white wine
- 2 cups freshly shelled English peas, blanched (see page 72)
- 1 cup pea stock (see page 72), chilled, or cold water
- 1 cup Fish Stock (see page 115), chilled
- 1 cup loosely packed fresh flat-leaf parsley leaves, blanched (see page 167)

- 1½ pounds monkfish tails, cut into 12 roughly 2-ounce medallions
- Sea salt and freshly ground pepper
- 1 cup Wondra flour, cake flour, or all-purpose flour
- 1 tablespoon plus 1 teaspoon olive oil
- 1 cup English peas, blanched (see page 72)
- 1 cup snow peas, blanched (see page 72)
- 1 cup snap peas, blanched (see page 72)
- 1½ teaspoons fresh lemon juice
- ½ cup Marcona almonds, roughly chopped
- 1 cup loosely packed pea shoots (optional)

MARMITAKO

TUNA, TOMATO, AND PEPPER STEW

Marmitako . . . it's fun to say! Sometimes that's enough to get the creative juices flowing. Paging through an old cookbook, the name caught my eye, but during the wrong time of year—the dead of winter, when local tomatoes and peppers were more than a season away. Then, several months later (I'm not making this up), on a rainy, early summer afternoon, I literally stepped on a local newspaper, the ink bleeding into the pavement, and got my shoe caught on the page. As I pulled the soggy section off my toe, a bolded word caught my eye: "Marmitako!" A recipe followed, but I left the ragged paper on the street and used my imagination to conjure up my own Basque summer stew.

Season the tuna pieces with salt and pepper on both sides. Let sit at room temperature while you prepare the rest of the stew.

Heat a large pot over medium-high heat and add the olive oil. When the oil begins to dance, add the bell peppers, whole jalapeño (if using), onion, and garlic. Sweat for 5 minutes, stirring occasionally. Add the tomatoes, potatoes, pimentón, and thyme and season with salt and black pepper. Cook for 1 minute, and pour in the sherry. Cook until the sherry is reduced by half, then add the fish stock. Bring to a simmer and cook gently for 15 minutes, or until the potatoes are tender. Taste and adjust the seasoning.

Add the tuna to the pot, pressing down on it gently to submerge in the stew. How long you cook the tuna depends on personal preference. Traditionally the tuna would be cooked through completely, but we like to leave the tuna rosy—closer to medium than well-done, and not completely cold and raw in the center (as tuna is often served). This takes about 4 minutes. To test, using tongs, fish a piece of tuna up to the surface of the stew. Using the tongs and a fork, see if you can gently rip the portion in half. If it doesn't let go willingly, it's still too rare. If you are able to gently pull the tuna apart, its color should still be pinkish. When they've achieved that sweet spot, transfer all of the tuna to to a plate to prevent it from cooking further.

Add the olives, parsley, and lemon juice to the stew and taste for seasoning one final time.

Using your hands, pull each of the 4 pieces of tuna into large chunks or flakes, so you are left with 16 pieces (or so). To serve, place 4 pieces of tuna at the bottom of each of four bowls and spoon the stew over the top. Finish each bowl with a drizzle of olive oil and a sprinkling of basil and serve immediately.

Serves 4

- 1 pound tuna, cut into 4 roughly 1-inch-thick planks
- Salt and freshly ground black pepper
- 2 tablespoons olive oil, plus more for drizzling
- 1 red bell pepper, seeded and cut into rings about ¼ inch thick
- 1 green bell pepper, seeded and cut into rings about ¼ inch thick
- 1 jalapeño (optional)
- 1 yellow onion, thinly sliced
- 5 cloves garlic, thinly sliced
- 2 cups roughly diced tomatoes
- 8 marble-sized waxy-skinned young (creamer) potatoes such as Yukon Gold, scrubbed and halved
- 1 teaspoon sweet pimentón
- 1 teaspoon chopped fresh thyme
- ½ cup fino sherry or dry white wine
- 3 cups Fish Stock (page 115)
- ¼ cup manzanilla or other briny green olives, pitted
- 2 tablespoons chopped fresh flat-leaf parsley
- Juice of ½ lemon
- 2 tablespoons torn fresh basil

CALAMARES RELLENOS
SQUID STUFFED WITH BLACK RICE

Here the famous black rice of Spain gets stuffed inside squid bodies, which are then pan-roasted. Minced chorizo makes an excellent addition to the stuffing, and aïoli could be served in place of—or along with—the piquillo vinaigrette. If you don't want to go to the trouble of stuffing the squid, you can cut the bodies into rings and fold them into the rice while it's cooking, with the last addition of stock.

Prepare the rice, then spread it out on a sheet pan and let cool for a few minutes on the countertop. Transfer to the refrigerator, uncovered, for at least 30 minutes and up to 2 days (cover with plastic wrap once cool).

While the rice is cooling, make the vinaigrette: Simply add all the ingredients to your blender and blend on high-speed until smooth.

Once the rice is cool, transfer it to a pastry bag fitted with a ½-inch round tip or a heavy-duty ziplock with one corner snipped off to create a roughly ½-inch opening. Pipe the rice into the squid bodies. You don't want to overstuff the squid, which may cause them to split or the stuffing to leak out during cooking. There should be enough rice inside each squid body that if you gently squeeze the squid, the filling reaches until about ¼ inch above the open end of the squid body. Using a toothpick, loosely skewer the opening of the squid to help contain the filling. (You can stuff the squid up to 1 day ahead and hold them, covered, in the fridge.)

Preheat the oven to 375°F.

Place a cast-iron or heavy-bottomed stainless-steel ovenproof sauté pan over medium heat. Season the stuffed squid lightly with salt. Add the olive oil to the hot pan, and then arrange the stuffed squid in the oil. Sear on the first side for 3 minutes. Flip each squid and transfer the pan to the oven. Roast until the stuffing is warm (you can use a cake tester or metal skewer to test the temperature by inserting it into the center of the squid for a few seconds, then removing the tester and pressing it against your wrist or lip—it should be warm), about 5 minutes. Remove from the oven and let rest for 3 minutes.

To serve, spoon a pool of the vinaigrette onto a serving plate and place the squid over the top. Drizzle with more vinaigrette and serve immediately.

Serves 4

Arroz Negro (page 114)

For the Piquillo Vinaigrette:
4 piquillo peppers, stemmed
2 tablespoons sherry vinegar
5 tablespoons olive oil
½ teaspoon fresh thyme leaves
 Salt

8 medium (4- to 6-inch-long) squid bodies, cleaned
 Sea salt
1 tablespoon olive oil

Gallegan fisherman's feast

BEVERAGE PAIRING

Txakoli

TETILLA

MEJILLONES EN ESCABECHE
37

PIMIENTOS DE PADRÓN
86

PULPO A LA GALLEGA
154

ARROZ MARINERO
112

Like nearly every region of Spain, the people of Galicia boast that the food on their table is the best in the country. While we will remain mum in that argument, it is fair to say that Galicia is Spain's seafood capital. The combination of the Atlantic, the nearby Mediterranean, and the local Rías Bixias have made the city of Vigo the largest fishing port in Europe. They are also known for the quality of their cattle and accordingly have some of Spain's finest cow's milk cheese—including a breast-shaped variety we've included on the menu called *tetilla*.

You can't go wrong with the local Albariño wines, but we love to drink fresh and zesty Basque Txakoli with a table of fish.

MERLUZA Y ALMEJAS EN SALSA VERDE

HAKE AND CLAMS IN GREEN SAUCE

Spaniards love parsley. Whereas Italian *salsa verde* usually has a half-dozen or so ingredients, and Mexican salsa verde is something entirely different, Spanish salsa verde is mostly a parsley sauce. We like to add some of the parsley during the cooking to get a more muted flavor and some at the end for a fresh, green finish. This dish merges a few of our favorite Basque fish recipes—Hake in Salsa Verde; Hake Cooked in Cider; and Clams with White Beans—combining three traditional recipes into one modern classic.

Season the hake with salt. Heat a large sauté pan with a tight-fitting lid over medium heat for 2 minutes. Add the olive oil to the hot pan, then arrange the hake fillets in the oil. Sear for 3 minutes. Add the garlic and sear the fish for 1 minute longer, letting the garlic toast without fussing.

Flip the fillets and add 2 tablespoons of the parsley, the cider, and the beans. Add the clams, discarding any that are open but do not close to the touch. Cover tightly and steam until the clams open, about 3 minutes. Lift the lid every 30 seconds or so to see if they have opened; depending on the type of clams, they could all open in 3 minutes, or it may take up to an additional 5 minutes.

Add the bean liquid or stock and bring to a bare simmer. Taste and add salt, if needed. (If you used white wine or a balanced cider, as opposed to the acidic Spanish variety, you might need to add a few drops of lemon juice at this point—a pat of butter certainly wouldn't hurt, either.) Finally stir in the remaining 2 tablespoons parsley. Discard any clams that failed to open.

Scoop into four shallow bowls or a large platter and serve immediately.

Serves 4

4	hake fillets, about 4 ounces each (you can substitute cod, halibut, or any firm white fish)
	Salt
2	tablespoons olive oil
2	cloves garlic, thinly sliced
4	tablespoons chopped fresh flat-leaf parsley
½	cup Spanish cider such as Isastegi, or any bone-dry cider or dry white wine
1	cup cooked white beans such as navy or cannellini
12	clams (we favor small varieties like cockles or Manilas), scrubbed and purged (page 38)
¼	cup bean cooking liquid (if you cooked the beans yourself), fish or chicken stock, or water

VIEIRAS A LA ZURRUKATUNA

SCALLOPS WITH CORN, TOMATOES, AND PEPPER SAUCE

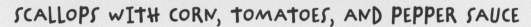

My sous chef, Jenni, came across a recipe for *zurrukatuna*, and, inspired by the author's notes, which explained that *zurrukatuna* is a Basque word meaning "a tasty or pleasant slurp," we ignored the traditional version (a salt-cod stew), and she worked on a dish we hoped would meet that definition. It's quite simple to prepare, but the scallops and peak-season corn and tomatoes make it luxurious. This dish, as much as any other in this book, finds the balance between Spanish and market-driven new American cooking.

To make the pepper sauce, preheat the oven to 425°F. Arrange all the peppers on a baking sheet and roast, turning once or twice as needed, until the skins are blistered and deeply charred, 15 to 20 minutes. Transfer the peppers to a bowl, cover tightly with plastic wrap, and let steam for 30 minutes.

While the peppers are steaming, bring a small saucepan of water to a boil and add 2 tablespoons salt. Prepare an ice-water bath by filling a large bowl with equal parts ice and water. Holding the stems by the ends, plunge the parsley leaves first into the boiling water (ideally the stems will not be submerged). After 30 seconds, plunge the parsley into the ice bath. Once cool, cut the stems off and squeeze as much water from the parsley leaves as possible. Set aside.

Warm a sauté pan over medium-high for 1 minute and add 1 tablespoon of the olive oil. Add the onion and garlic, reduce the heat to medium, and cook for 10 minutes, stirring occasionally. Stir in 1 teaspoon salt, then add the wine and deglaze the pan, using a wooden spoon to scrape up any browned bits on the bottom of the pan. Cook until the wine has reduced by half, about 3 minutes. The onion should have sweated down and softened, but should not yet be caramelized.

Peel the peppers, discarding the stems and seeds. Put the peppers and any juice that remains in the bowl to a blender. Add the blanched parsley, onion, garlic, remaining ½ cup olive oil, and another 1 teaspoon salt. Blend until smooth. Taste to see if more salt is needed. Cover to keep warm and set aside. (You can let the sauce cool and refrigerate, tightly covered, for up to 3 days. Reheat gently to serve.)

Heat a sauté pan over medium-high heat for 2 minutes. Add 1 tablespoon of the olive oil to the hot pan and then the corn. Cook for 3 minutes, stirring once or twice. Add the tomatoes, cooking for just 20 seconds to barely warm them, while not allowing them to break down. Remove from the heat and stir in the lemon juice, parsley, and salt and black pepper to taste (start with 1 teaspoon of salt and a couple cracks of pepper). Set aside while you cook the scallops.

Serves 4

For the pepper sauce:

2	cubanelle peppers
1	green bell pepper
	Salt
1	small bunch fresh flat-leaf parsley
1	tablespoon plus ½ cup olive oil
½	Spanish onion, thinly sliced
2	cloves garlic, thinly sliced
1	cup dry white wine

2	tablespoons olive oil
	Kernels from 2 ears of corn (see Note)
12	cherry tomatoes, halved
1	tablespoon fresh lemon juice
1	tablespoon chopped fresh flat-leaf parsley
	Salt and freshly ground black pepper
12	large sea scallops
8	fresh basil leaves, torn into roughly 4 pieces each

Heat a heavy-bottomed sauté pan (cast-iron works well for this) over high heat for 3 minutes. (If your pan isn't large enough to comfortably fit all 12 scallops without crowding, you will need to cook them in two batches or two pans.) Season both sides of the scallops with salt and black pepper. Add the remaining 1 tablespoon olive oil to the pan (it may smoke a bit) and quickly add the scallops. Let them cook untouched (this is important) for 3 minutes. Gently lift a few of the scallops and peek at the bottom. If they still look a bit blond, allow them to cook on that side for another minute or two. When the scallops are deeply browned on the first side, flip and cook for 2 more minutes. Using tongs, gently transfer to a plate.

To serve, spoon some sauce into each of four shallow bowls. Arrange 3 scallops in each on top of the sauce. Top with the corn and tomato mixture, dividing it evenly. Finally, scatter the torn basil over the top. Serve immediately—pleasant slurps are best enjoyed warm!

NOTE: *Our recommended method for removing the kernels from an ear of corn is to place a kitchen towel on the bottom of a large bowl (not a fragile one). Stand up the corn so that the wider end of the cob is resting securely on the towel. Slowly work your knife down the side of the cob, following the contour while you remove the kernels, which will fall into the bowl. Rotate the cob and repeat until all the kernels are stripped from the cob (you can save the cobs to make Corn Flan on page 185).*

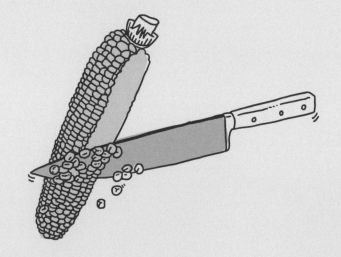

SuQueT

CATALAN FISH STEW

Any coastal city tends to have their version of fish stew: there's *bouillabaisse* in Marseille, *cioppino* in San Francisco, clam chowder in New England, and in and around Barcelona, you'll find the Catalan *suquet*. As in most of the stews above, the fish used may vary, but all have a defining characteristic; in *suquet*, it's the use of almonds to thicken and enrich the broth. The somewhat surprising combination of nuts and fish is what initially led to my interest in this dish, but after eating it a few times, it became clear why it's a classic.

If you purchase or have premade the fish stock, this is a quick stew to make.

Place a sauté pan over medium heat and add 1 tablespoon of the olive oil, the onion, and the garlic. Sweat for 10 minutes, stirring occasionally. Add 2 tablespoons of the parsley, the saffron, and the pimentón and toast for 1 minute, allowing the spices to bloom. Add the wine and deglaze the pan, using a wooden spoon to scrape up any browned bits sticking to the bottom of the pan. Cook until the wine has reduced by half, then add 1 cup of the fish stock and bring to a simmer and stir to mix well.

Transfer half the contents of the pan to a blender. Add the almonds and process until smooth. Set aside.

Add the remaining 1 cup fish stock, the shrimp stock, and the tomatoes with their juices to the pot with the remaining sauce base, crushing the tomatoes by hand as you add them. Season with a pinch of salt, add the potatoes, return the sauce to a simmer, and cook until until the potatoes are tender, about 15 minutes.

Once the potatoes are tender, add the cod, mussels, and clams, discarding any shellfish that are open and do not close to the touch. Cover the pot tightly and steam for 3 minutes. Add the squid and peas and gently stir in the almond paste. Cook for another 2 minutes, or until the clams and mussels are open. Once they are, remove from the heat and stir in the shrimp and the remaining 1 tablespoon parsley. (Discard any shellfish that failed to open.) Allow the shrimp to cook in the residual heat for 90 seconds. Taste the broth and adjust with salt and lemon juice if it needs a hit of acid.

Serve immediately, with the crusty bread.

Serves 4

1	tablespoon olive oil
1	yellow onion, diced
2	cloves garlic, thinly sliced
3	tablespoons chopped fresh flat-leaf parsley
1	teaspoon saffron threads
½	teaspoon sweet pimentón
½	cup dry white wine
2	cups Fish Stock (page 115)
½	cup Marcona almonds
1	cup shrimp stock (using the shells from below) or fish stock
½	cup canned whole plum tomatoes, with their juice
	Sea salt
6	marble-sized young (creamer) waxy-skinned potatoes such as Yukon Gold, scrubbed and quartered
8	ounces cod or other flaky white fish, cut into 8 pieces total
12	mussels, scrubbed and debearded
12	clams (Manila or littleneck are good choices), scrubbed and purged (see page 38)
4	squid, cleaned, bodies cut into 1-inch rings, legs whole
1	cup English peas, fresh or frozen
12	large (21/25 count) shrimp (about ½ pound), peeled (shells saved) and deveined
	Fresh lemon juice, if needed
	Crusty bread for serving

Trucha a la Sal
Con Tres Salsas

TROUT BAKED IN A SALT CRUST WITH ROMESCO, SALPICÓN, AND AÏOLI VERDE

This is a simple technique used all over the world, and makes for an impressive display in addition to being delicious. Brook trout is abundant both in Spain and domestically, and the typical size of around 1 pound is an ideal size for cooking and serving whole. One of our motivations for putting this on the menu was to have a theatrical dish that we could present to our guests before plating. This works at home as well. After the fish has baked and cooled a bit, you can crack the salt crust and give your guests a peek at what they're in store for. There is no end to what sauces can be served alongside, but we find that the trio here presents three distinct and delicious options that speak to and of Spain.

In addition to the three sauces, we like to serve this fish dish with a salad and roasted potatoes. The recipe is easily multiplied; just add a trout for every two or three diners. Unless you're catching your own, your fishmonger will do the cleaning (gutting and scaling). In addition, while it's not necessary, I highly recommend having the trout butterflied and deboned by your fishmonger. If they are unwilling, it does require a bit of time and you can certainly forgo this step. At the restaurant, this allows us to quickly unpack and serve the fish during a busy dinner service, but the bones can be removed after baking.

To make the salpicón, in a food processor, combine all of the ingredients and pulse until a coarse, loose paste is formed. Set aside.

To make the Aïoli Verde, in a blender, combine the garlic, parsley, scallion tops, and olive oil and process until well blended and smooth. Add the Aïoli and blend until well combined. Set aside.

Make the romesco as directed and set aside.

Preheat the oven to 425°F.

Cut the top and bottom off the lemon. Slice top-to-bottom into thin slices (discarding the first slice, which is mostly peel), until you've reach the middle of the lemon (you should have 4 to 6 slices). Set the slices aside and cut the remaining lemon half into 4 wedges. Remove the seeds from the wedges and reserve to serve with the finished dish.

Place half the lemon slices, half the scallions, and half the fennel fronds into the cavity of each of the 2 trout.

Line two baking sheets with foil. In a large bowl, combine the salt and water to achieve the feel of loose, wet sand. Using about one-third of the salt mixture, line each tray with enough salt to create a base for the fish. Press lightly into the tray to pack the mixture. Place one trout on each tray on top of the salt and cover with the remainder of salt mixture. Press and pack the salt around the fish to cover completely and evenly. The crust will remain a bit delicate—the steam created by the cooking of the fish will create a stronger structure as the fish cooks. Carefully place the fish in the oven and bake for 22 minutes (if your trout is more than 1 pound, add an additional minute for every additional ounce).

Remove from the oven and let cool for 5 minutes. After 5 minutes, using a heavy spoon or the back of a sturdy knife, give the salt crust a few firm taps to crack it (try to work along the edges of the hidden fish). Carefully remove a few large chunks of salt to expose the fish and let cool for an additional 5 minutes. At this point you can show your guests the fish peeking from the salt for a theatrical dinner interlude.

Next remove the trout completely from the salt crust and dust off any salt that remains. If your trout has been butterflied and deboned, you can serve immediately, opening the fish and placing the entire trout skin-side down on a serving plate.

If your fish is not deboned, place on a cutting board or large plate and use a butter knife to make a gentle incision just above the spine. Work the knife down, wiggling it slowly, and then using a spatula remove the top fillet from the bone. The spine will now be exposed and the head and spine can be pulled away, exposing the bottom fillet. The only bones that remain are the pin bones, of which there are many. You can either remove them at this point, or serve and let your guests know that bones remain.

Serve the fish whole on a platter, drizzled with the olive oil and with the reserved 4 lemon wedges on the side. Serve the trio of sauces each in their own bowl and allow your guests to dress their fish as desired.

Serves 4

For the salpicón:

½ cup cornichons

½ cup guindilla peppers or peperoncini (see page 17)

½ cup manzanilla or other briny green olives, pitted

½ cup olive oil

1 tablespoon fennel fronds

1 tablespoon fresh flat-leaf parsley leaves

For the Aïoli Verde:

½ clove garlic

1 small bunch fresh flat-leaf parsley

2 scallions, tender green parts only

½ cup olive oil

½ cup Aïoli (page 80)

Romesco Sauce (page 143), processed until coarse, for serving

1 lemon

4 scallions

2 stalks fennel, with feathery tops

2 whole brook trout, about 1 pound each, cleaned

3 pounds kosher salt

4 cups water

2 teaspoons olive oil

POSTRES

DESSERTS ARE PERHAPS

the lone category of traditional Spanish cuisine that lacks depth. A short list of classics dominates the sweets scene in Spain, with the familiar rice puddings, flans, and churros occupying the bulk of dessert menus. True to our approach to their savory counterparts, in some cases we prepare our straightforward take on a classic, but other times we have used tradition as a jumping-off point to create a recipe that brings the best of Spanish and American cooking together. Our Migas Dulces or "Sweet Crumbs," for example, combines a Spanish method of using leftover bread with the American classic strawberry shortcake to create something simple, yet new and delicious. We have no pastry chef at the restaurant, which means that our desserts tend to be easy to prepare and simple to serve. Flavor and texture are paramount rather than technique and creativity. As a result, no matter the season or occasion, our roster of desserts provides an easy and satisfying way to end a meal.

CHURROS CON CHOCOLATE

CHURROS WITH CHOCOLATE SAUCE

It's hard to think of a sweet or pastry in North America with as much cultural significance as the churro has in Spain. There are really very few foods here that we associate equally with starting our day and ending it (churros are a favorite both on the way to work and after a night out). Naturally we wanted to serve churros, but as is so often the case, the simplest things prove the most difficult and we tweaked the recipe for over a year before nailing it.

To make the churro batter, in a saucepan over medium heat, combine the butter and water and heat gently to melt the butter. Once melted, add the flour, salt, and sugar and whisk until well blended. Transfer to a bowl and letcool for 3 or 4 minutes. Add the beaten eggs and, using a wooden spoon, work the eggs into the dough until well blended, smooth, and shiny. This takes several minutes (and some arm strength). Let cool in the bowl before using.

To make the chocolate sauce, simply combine the chocolate and cream in a small saucepan over low heat and melt together, whisking occasionally until smooth and well blended. Set aside at room temperature until ready to use.

To make the churros, pour oil into a deep fryer or heavy-bottomed 4-quart saucepan to a depth of 4 inches and heat to 375°F. Put the sugar in a large, shallow bowl and place nearby.

Spoon the batter into a pastry bag fitted with a large (we use #7) "open-star" pastry tip. Carefully pipe the churros into the fryer, a few at a time and each 5 to 6 inches long, and cook until they are a deep golden brown, about 5 minutes. Use a spider or slotted spoon to turn the churros over once or twice to ensure even cooking. Transfer to paper towels to drain, then toss in the sugar. The residual heat and bit of oil will help the sugar stick (if too much sticks, knock off any excess). Repeat to make the remaining churros.

Serve at once, or keep warm in a very low oven until serving.

**Makes about forty
5- to 6-inch churros**

For the churro batter:

7	tablespoons unsalted butter
¾	cup plus 2 tablespoons water
¾	cup plus 2 tablespoons all-purpose flour
1	teaspoon kosher salt
1	teaspoon sugar
3	medium or 2 extra-large eggs, lightly beaten

For the chocolate sauce:

8	ounces bittersweet chocolate coins (we use Guittard 72 percent cacao)
2	cups heavy cream

	Canola oil for frying
2	cups sugar

QUESADILLA con UVAS

MINI GOAT CHEESECAKES WITH CONCORD GRAPES

On a late summer morning while I was walking through the Union Square farmers' market, the sweet smell of Concord grapes caught my attention. I was reminded of an experiment that I had been meaning to try—to flash-fry grapes to peel them, just as we do with cherry tomatoes for the Salpicón (page 151) and Salmarejo (page 79). The experiment was a success. In addition to being a quick way to peel the grapes, I was able to remove the skins in one dramatic piece and fry them further to create tannic "chips," which balance these rich cakes and provide a welcome crunch. (Make sure to buy the seedless variety.) This recipe, inspired by one in Jose Pizarro's *Spanish Flavors*, proved the ideal stage to show off the grapes.

To prepare the grapes, pour oil into a deep fryer or heavy-bottomed 4-quart saucepan to a depth of 3 inches and heat to 375°F. Working in small batches, add the grapes handful at a time to the hot oil. In 15 to 30 seconds, the grapes should float to the top and you should see the skins beginning to split and separate from the interiors. Use a spider or slotted spoon, transfer the grapes to paper towels to drain.

Once cool enough to handle, gently remove the skins from the grapes. Return the skins to the fryer, again working in batches, and fry until crisp, about 30 seconds. Drain on paper towels and set aside at room temperature.

Put about one-third of the peeled grapes in a blender and add the sugar and sherry. Blend until smooth. Transfer the grape sauce to a small saucepan over medium heat and bring to a simmer. Cook until reduced by half, about 3 minutes. Remove from the heat, let cool to room temperature, and add the remaining grapes to the sauce. Let cool slightly, then cover and refrigerate until ready to serve.

To make the cake, preheat the oven to 325°F. Have ready six 3-inch silicone cakes molds. (If you don't have silicone molds, you can bake the cakes in disposable 3-inch ramekins sprayed with nonstick cooking spray.)

Using a stand mixer or hand mixer, in a bowl, beat the cheeses together. Add the sugar, cornstarch, salt, eggs, and sour cream and beat until a light, uniform texture is reached. Pour the batter into the baking molds. Place the filled molds on a baking sheet and bake for 25 to 35 minutes, or until a toothpick inserted into the center of a cake comes out clean. Let the cakes cool at room temperature for at least 30 minutes before unmolding. Once unmolded, hold the cakes in the refrigerator.

About 30 minutes before serving, remove the cakes and grapes from the fridge to let come to room temperature. To serve, place a cake in the center of each plate. Spoon out a few grapes from the sauce and place on each cake; put a few off to the side of the cakes too, with a bit of the sauce. Finally, place 3 crispy grape skins around each plate and serve.

Serves 6

For the grapes:

Canola oil for frying

½ pound seedless Concord grapes

¼ cup sugar

¼ cup cream, amontillado, or oloroso sherry

For the cake:

8 ounces cream cheese, at room temperature

8 ounces goat cheese, at room temperature

⅔ cup sugar

1½ tablespoons cornstarch

½ teaspoon salt

2 large eggs

½ cup sour cream

SWEET MIGAS

SWEET CROUTONS WITH STRAWBERRIES AND WHIPPED CREAM

As a restaurant without a pastry chef, we're always looking for ways to provide a sweet finish without measuring, kneading, sifting, or baking. In late May, New York's farmers' markets see the first fresh fruit of the year—strawberries—and our work gets a lot easier. This dessert, our take on strawberry shortcake, works with any berry or any juicy stone fruit. We use leftover baguette, but you could make the dessert a bit more luxurious by starting with challah or brioche. For an equally decadent but somewhat healthier version, substitute Greek yogurt (full- or low-fat) for the cream.

Line a baking sheet with a wire rack or paper towels.

Tear the bread into roughly 1-inch chunks. In a large frying pan over medium heat, melt the butter. As soon as the butter is melted and beginning to foam, add the torn bread. Toast the bread in the foaming butter for about 5 minutes, swirling the pan and stirring the bread every 30 seconds or so. The bread should be lightly browned, but not completely dry in the center. Using a slotted spoon, transfer the bread to a bowl. Toss with 2 tablespoons of the sugar, then spread the croutons on the prepared baking sheet to cool.

Cut one-third of the berries into small to medium dice (about ¼ inch) and put in a bowl. Add 2 tablespoons of the sugar and toss to coat. Let stand at room temperature for at least 30 minutes to draw juice from the berries.

Using a stand mixer or hand mixer, in a bowl, whip the cream with the remaining 1 tablespoon sugar and the vanilla. Whip until soft peaks form.

Cut the remaining berries into quarters and toss with the diced and macerated strawberries and their juice.

To plate, haphazardly layer the whipped cream, croutons, and berries on small plates or in shallow bowls. Drizzle the strawberry juice over the top and serve.

Serves 4

1 small or ½ large day-old baguette, crust removed

6 tablespoons unsalted butter

5 tablespoons sugar

1 pint strawberries, hulled

2 cups heavy cream

1 teaspoon vanilla extract

FLAN

BAKED CUSTARD

Often after a big meal, the last thing you want to think about is more food. But you gather the "courage" to have just a taste of dessert, and sometimes that's all you can muster . . . or you fight your way through a few more rich and decadent bites. Flan is one of those desserts that you don't have to fight. Just slightly sweet, it's light and mild—the sort of finish to a meal that's a relief.

Preheat the oven to 350°F. (If you have a convection or fan function, turn it off.) Place eight 3-inch shallow ramekins, cazuelas, or small ovenproof custard bowls in a large baking dish with sides at least as deep as the ramekins.

In a small saucepan over medium heat, gently warm the milk to a simmer, stirring with a rubber spatula to prevent the milk from scorching. While it heats, in a heat-proof bowl, whisk together the eggs and egg yolks and ½ cup of the sugar.

When the milk has come to a simmer, remove from the heat and temper it into the egg mixture by adding the milk gradually while whisking constantly to avoid scrambling the eggs. Set aside. Heat 8 cups water to a boil in a pot (if you have an electric kettle, this is a perfect time to use it).

In a small saucepan, combine the remaining ½ cup sugar and a few drops of water (about 1 teaspoon). Stir together with a rubber spatula or a spoon. Place over medium heat and allow the sugar to caramelize. Resist the urge to stir, but you can roll the pan gently once or twice if the sugar is beginning to caramelize unevenly. When the sugar has melted and begun to bubble, turn the heat down to low and let it it cook to a deep golden brown. When the desired color is reached, stir again to make sure the sugar is completely melted. Remove from the heat and, working quickly before the sugar cools and solidifies, pour the caramel into the bottom of the ramekins, dividing it evenly among the eight dishes. As you pour, gently lift and rotate the ramekins to coat the entire bottom of each dish. After about a minute, the caramel will have cooled and become a solid base.

Gently ladle the custard into each ramekin on top of the caramel, dividing it evenly. Carefully place the baking dish containing the flans in the oven and, with the door still open, pour the hot water into the baking dish to come halfway up the sides of the ramekins, creating a water bath. Bake until set, 15 to 20 minutes.

Remove the pan from the oven and let cool for a few minutes. Serve warm, or to serve cold, transfer the ramekins to a small baking sheet and place the custards in the refrigerator until well chilled, about 1 hour. Or cover tightly with plastic wrap and refrigerate for up to 3 days. To unmold, run a butter knife along the side of the dish, place a small plate on top, and flip the flan out. The caramel on the bottom should help them unmold cleanly. Serve immediately.

**Makes eight
3-inch custards**

2   cups milk
4   large eggs plus 2 egg yolks
1   cup sugar

MEL I MATÓ

HONEY AND FRESH CHEESE

When it comes time to talk dessert with our guests, the first question is, would they like something sweet or would they prefer cheese? Often they are craving a bit of both, but lack ample appetite. Mel i Mató is the answer. A traditional Catalan dessert, *mel* is Catalan for "honey" and *mató* is a local style of farmers' cheese. Usually accompanied by nuts, our version, which is somewhat firmer than the traditional ricottalike texture, lies somewhere between cheese and cake. Traditionally the dish has no salt, but we like to finish the plate with a few grains of flaky sea salt—you can leave that choice up to your guests.

If you want to make the dessert a bit more elaborate, add some seasonal fruit on top as well—strawberries, peaches, grapes, apples, and many more would be nice; as would practically any dried fruit. A simple finish, perfect for entertaining.

This recipe calls for nonhomogenized milk, sometimes called "creamline," which allows curds to form more easily when making the cheese. If you aren't up for making your own cheese, substitute 1 pound ricotta.

In a saucepan, warm the milk to a simmer very gently over low heat to prevent the milk from scorching or boiling over.

Just when the milk comes to a simmer, remove from the heat and stir in the lemon juice. Stir gently as the milk separates and the curds begin to form. Line a colander or strainer with a couple layers of cheesecloth and pour the milk through into the sink. The curds and whey will be mostly separated immediately. Nest the cheese in the colander over a bowl for at least 20 minutes to let the whey continue to drain. The longer you allow it to drain, the firmer the cheese will become—it's a matter of taste.

You could serve the cheese warm, but more likely you'll want to have the cheese ready to go, in which case you can place the cheese in an airtight container in the refrigerator. It will be best the first day or two, but will last for several more days after that.

To serve, scoop a few spoons of the cheese onto a serving plate or individual plates and top with honey to taste and nuts. If you like, you can also finish with a few flakes of crunchy salt.

Serves 4

½ gallon whole nonhomogenized (creamline) milk

Juice of 2 lemons

4 to 8 tablespoons honey

½ cup walnuts (or pecans, pine nuts, almonds, hazelnuts . . .)

Sea salt (optional)

FLAN DE MAÍZ

CORN FLAN

Flan is certainly one of the staple desserts of Spain, and there are endless ways to flavor the custard itself and any number of toppings—syrups, compotes, sauces—that can be served alongside. This variation was initially developed as a use for the corncobs that had been stripped of their kernels for our Vieiras a la Zurrukatuna (page 167), but you can leave the kernels on if you don't have another use for them. As it's a summery variation of flan, we like to top it with blueberry compote, another seasonal treat.

The key to this dish is getting the milk to taste of corn, and the best way to do that is to make the corn milk the day before you want to make the flan.

The day before you plan to make the flan, cut the cobs into a few large chunks, place in a small saucepan, and pour in the milk. Bring to a simmer, then remove from the heat and let cool. Once cool, transfer to an airtight container and refrigerator overnight. The next day, strain out the corn. Some milk will be trapped in the cobs, but you should have at least 2 cups of milk that smells and tastes of corn.

Preheat the oven to 350°F. (If you have a convection or fan function, turn it off.) Place eight 3-inch shallow ramekins, cazuelas, or small ovenproof custard bowls in a large baking dish with sides at least as deep as the ramekins.

Bring 2 cups of the corn milk to a simmer in a small saucepan very gently over low heat to prevent the milk from scorching or boiling over. While it heats, in a bowl, whisk together the eggs, egg yolks, and ½ cup of the sugar.

When the milk has come to a simmer, remove from the heat and temper it into the egg mixture. This means that you will add just a few drops of milk at first, while whisking constantly; this will begin to heat the eggs and sugar without scrambling the eggs. Add the milk little by little, still whisking constantly. Once you have added all the milk and the custard is smooth and well blended, set aside.

Heat 8 cups water to a boil in a pot (if you have an electric kettle, this is a perfect time to use it).

In a small saucepan, bring the maple syrup to a simmer and cook until reduced by half, about 5 minutes. Remove from the heat and, working quickly while the syrup is nice and liquidy, pour it into the bottom of the ramekins, dividing it evenly among the eight dishes. As you pour, gently lift and rotate the ramekins to coat the entire bottom of each dish.

Gently ladle the corn custard into each ramekin on top of the syrup, dividing it evenly. Carefully place the baking dish containing the flans in the oven and, with the door still open, pour the hot water into the baking dish to come halfway up the sides of the ramekins, creating a water bath. Bake until set, 15 to 20 minutes.

While the flan is baking, in a small saucepan combine the blueberries with the lemon juice, the remaining 2 tablespoons sugar, and ½ cup water. Place over medium-low heat and cook, stirring occasionally, until the berries burst and the mixture thickens, about 10 minutes. Let the compote cool. (The compote may be made in advance and kept covered in the refrigerator for at least 2 days.)

Remove the pan from the oven and let cool for a few minutes. Serve warm, or to serve cold, transfer the ramekins to a small baking sheet and place the custards in the refrigerator until well chilled, about 1 hour. Or cover tightly with plastic wrap and refrigerate for up to 3 days. To unmold, run a butter knife along the side of the dish, place a small plate on top, and flip the flan out. The syrup on the bottom should help them unmold cleanly. Serve immediately, with a heaping spoonful of blueberry compote draped over half of each flan, falling off to one side of the plate.

Makes eight 3-inch custards

2	corncobs, stripped of their kernels (see recipe introduction)
2½	cups milk
4	large egg plus 2 egg yolks
½	cup plus 2 tablespoons sugar
¼	cup maple syrup
1	pint blueberries
1	tablespoon lemon juice

TORRIJAS CON MERMELADA

SPANISH "FRENCH" TOAST WITH BITTER ORANGE

What distinguishes *torrijas* from a more typical French toast is that after soaking in custard, these sweet toasts are deep-fried. This creates a crisp exterior and a fluffy, almost doughnut-like interior. Deep-frying can be a hassle at home, but a good alternative is pan-frying or shallow frying. Instead of completely submerging the item being fried, pan-frying uses a sauté or frying pan with deep sides; only an inch or two of oil is required and works well for this recipe since the toast is flipped during frying anyway.

Note that you have to start the torrijas the night before to give the bread a good soaking in the custard. Serve these toasts with any sort of syrup, jam, whipped cream, or cheese—experiment to find a combination of your own.

To make the marmalade, cut the oranges into quarters, then slice each quarter into thin pieces. Working over a bowl to catch the juices, remove the seeds.

Using a paring knife (not a vegetable peeler), cut the peel and pith off the juice orange (discard them), exposing just the flesh. Chop the orange roughly, then remove the seeds, again catching the juices in the bowl.

Place all of the oranges in a large pot and add water to cover. Bring to a simmer over high heat, reduce the heat to low, and cook gently for 1 hour. After an hour, add the granulated sugar and glucose, if using, and continue to cook until the marmalade is quite thick and sticky, about 2 hours longer. To test, place a spoonful on a chilled plate. Allow it to cool for about 1 minute, and then run your finger through it. The streak made by your finger should remain, without the marmalade running over it.

Transfer the warm marmalade to a storage container and let cool uncovered until it has reached room temperature. It will keep, tightly covered in the fridge, for up to 3 months.

To make the torrijas, in a bowl, whisk together all of the ingredients except the bread. Place the bread in a baking dish and pour the custard over it to cover. Wrap the dish with plastic and soak in the refrigerator overnight.

The following day, remove the bread from the custard (most of the custard will have been absorbed). Pour canola oil into a deep fryer or heavy-bottomed 4-quart pot to a depth of 4 inches (or shallow-fry, see note above) and heat over medium-high heat to 375°F. Fry the toasts in batches until golden and crispy, using tongs to turn them when they are golden on one side, about 3 minutes per side. Using the tongs or a skimmer, transfer to paper towels to drain.

Let cool slightly, then dust with the powdered sugar. Serve at room temperature with the marmalade.

NOTE: *No need to use glucose, but it adds a stickiness and sheen that is desirable in a marmalade.*

Serves 4

For the Bitter Orange Marmalade:

- 1 pound bitter (Seville) oranges, scrubbed
- 1 juice orange such as Valencia, or 1 navel orange
- 1 cup granulated sugar
- 3 tablespoons glucose or more granulated sugar (see Note)

For the torrijas:

- 2 large eggs
- 1 large egg yolk
- 2/3 cup milk
-     Zest of ½ orange
- ½ teaspoon freshly grated nutmeg
- 1 teaspoon ground cinnamon
- 1 tablespoon pastry flour or all-purpose flour
- 1 teaspoon cornstarch
- ½ teaspoon baking powder
- 3 tablespoons sparkling water
- 2 tablespoons sugar
- 1 baguette, crusts removed, cut into roughly 8 planks about 1 by 2 by 3 inches

Canola oil for frying

Powdered sugar for dusting

BEBiDAS

DRINKING IS INGRAINED in the culinary tradition of Spain, in the best of ways. In Spain, drinking elevates the social experience of eating. It is a rarity to see Spanish food being enjoyed without a crisp glass of white or a chilled red wine, an easy-drinking lager beer served as cold as it gets, or what we like to call a *refresco*—a simple mixed drink of wine or beer with soda. Unabashedly, we mix red wine and cola to create the Basque favorite beach drink, Kalimotxo. With pride, we developed our own vermouth recipes, and pour them on draft to fully re-create the experience of drinking homemade vermouth in the tapas bar of Madrid. With our cocktail program, we've elevated the under-appreciated fortified wines, vermouth, and sherry by mixing them with spirits. Finally, we've taken Spain's Gin and Tonic obsession to the next level, developing our own tonic recipe and serving it cold and carbonated from a tap.

REFRESCOS

SPANISH WINE AND BEER COOLERS

If you visit Spain, you will find that traditionally, the Spanish people drink all day long. In an effort to stay even-keeled over the course of the day and night, there is a tradition of mixing beer and wine with soda to take the edge off. Each region of the country has their own local spin, and we brought them all to NYC. We like to call them *refrescos*, which translates to "refreshments." These easy-drinking wine and beer coolers are the perfect way to start a meal, or just sip all day in the park.

Refrescos are also amazing party drinks—they are fun, easy to make in pitchers, and, if you've got a powerful blender (or a slushie machine), make for awesome frozen cocktails.

Notes: In true NYC fashion, we give everyone the opportunity to add liquor to their refrescos, and in each recipe we note which spirit we think is best. Also, all the recipes make one glass, but for a larger batch, multiply the recipe as many times as you like.

KALIMOTXO

RED WINE AND COCA-COLA

Also known as "Poor Man's Sangria," Kalimotxo is the drink of choice for the Basque Country's youth. All it requires is a one-euro bottle of red wine and a one-liter bottle of cola. As a beach drink, the cool kids simply pour out half the cola bottle, fill it to the top with wine, and serve over ice. At the restaurant, we spice it up a bit with bitters and lemon juice, but we still present it in a glass Coke bottle tableside, for fun. We also do an atypical white version of the drink with white wine, Sprite, and lime.

5   oz red wine (we like Tempranillo)
5   oz Coca-Cola
3   lemon wedges
2   dashes of Angostura bitters
     Ice
     Optional: 1 oz dark rum

Combine the wine and cola in a pint glass. Squeeze in the juice of 2 of the lemon wedges and add the bitters. Add ice and stir well. Garnish with the remaining lemon wedge and serve.

AGUA DE VALENCIA

SPARKLING WINE AND ORANGE SODA

It's no surprise that the local drink, or "water of Valencia," is made with oranges and cava, the well-known Spanish sparkling wine. The province of Valencia is famous for its oranges, and is also located on the Mediterranean coast just south of Catalunya, the main cava-producing region. We make our own orange syrup, but if you don't have time, just top with a bit of orange Fanta; after all, that's what the Spanish do. This drink is like a mimosa, but better.

Pour the wine, vermouth, and Orange Syrup into a rocks glass. Add ice and stir well. Garnish with the orange twist and serve.

3½	oz cava or other sparkling white wine
¾	oz sweet white vermouth such as Cocchi Americano
½	oz Orange Syrup (recipe follows)
	Ice
	Orange twist for garnish
	Optional: 1 oz vodka

ORANGE SYRUP

In a saucepan over high heat, combine all of the ingredients. Bring to a simmer and cook gently for 20 minutes, stirring every once in a while, until the sugar dissolves. Refrigerate in sealed quart containers. Will last for up to 2 weeks.

Makes 3 quarts

	Zest and juice of 8 oranges
8	cups white sugar
10	cups water
2	tablespoons citric acid powder

TINTO DE VERANO

RED VERMOUTH AND CITRUS SODA

Tinto de Verano translates to "red wine of summer," named so because adding "gaseosa"—a citrus soda only found in Spain that's so addictive we had to find a way to make in ourselves—is the most refreshing way to drink red wine. As a result, it is often served in the summer. The Spaniards consider sangria to be way too commercial, and so do we. At our restaurant, we substitute Tinto de Verano for sangria and our house red vermouth for red wine to make the mixture more complex and give our guests an easy way to fall in love with vermouth. For this one, we highly suggest adding spirits, as there is no better complement to our red vermouth than gin.

2 oz Red Vermouth (page 203), or any Spanish red vermouth or red wine

½ oz Citric Syrup (recipe follows) or Sprite Zero

Ice

2 oz soda water

Orange twist for garnish

Optional: 1 ounce gin

Pour the vermouth and Citric Syrup into a rocks glass. Add add ice and stir well. Top with the soda water, garnish with the orange twist, and serve.

CITRIC SYRUP

Combine the water, sugar, and citric acid in a saucepan. Bring to a boil over high heat and reduce the heat to maintain a simmer. Stir until the sugar dissolves, 4 to 6 minutes. Remove from the heat and let cool. Cover and store refrigerated for up to a month.

Makes 1 quart

2 cups hot water

2 cups sugar

5 teaspoons citric acid

CLARA

LIGHT BEER AND LEMON SODA

Clara con limón, or *clara* for short, is the easiest of all the *refrescos* to describe: It is simply what the Spanish call a Shandy. *Clara* is slang for light beer; *con limón* means, of course, "with lemon." It is our favorite shift drink, because it quenches the after-work thirst better than anything else in the world. Add a float of soda water if you want it to be extra fizzy.

Pour the beer, Simple Syrup, and lemon juice into a pint glass. Add ice slowly (be careful not to spill beer over the top), then stir. Garnish with the lemon wedge and serve.

10	oz light beer (the Spanish use Estrella, we like to use our staff's favorite shift beer, Miller High Life)
¾	oz Simple Syrup (recipe follows)
¾	oz fresh lemon juice
	Ice
	Lemon wedge for garnish
	Optional: 1 oz bourbon

SIMPLE SYRUP

Combine the sugar and water in a saucepan and heat gently over medium heat, stirring occasionally to help dissolve the sugar. When the sugar is dissolved, about 5 minutes, remove from the heat and let cool. Store in an airtight container in the refrigerator for up to 1 month.

Makes 2 cups

1	cup sugar
1	cup water

RebuJiTo

DRY SHERRY AND GINGER SODA

The Rebujito is the *refresco* most popular in the south of Spain, in the province of Andulusia also known as sherry country. The Rebujito's name comes from the Spanish verb *arrebujar*, meaning "to jumble up." In our opinion, the Rebujito is the simplest, most refreshing sherry cocktail around. The easiest way to make this mixed drink is with equal parts ginger ale and dry sherry, with a wedge of lime to squeeze. We make it a little fresher and a little more delicious by using a house ginger syrup. Add dark rum to the Rebujito and you'll have yourself a sherry-infused Dark and Stormy.

Combine the sherry, Ginger Syrup, and lime juice in a cocktail shaker. Fill with ice and shake well. Strain into a Collins glass, fill with clean ice, and top with the soda water and bitters. (If want to add rum, leave space at the top of the glass.) Garnish with the lime wedge and serve.

2 oz manzanilla or any fino-style sherry

¾ oz Ginger Syrup (recipe follows)

¾ oz fresh lime juice

Ice

2 dashes of Angostura bitters

2 oz soda water (can sub with ginger beer if you don't make the ginger syrup)

Lime wedge for garnish

Optional: 1 oz dark rum

GINGER SYRUP

Using a vegetable juicer, juice the ginger. (If you don't have a vegetable juicer, in a blender, buzz the ginger on high speed.) Strain the juice through a fine-mesh strainer. Add the sugar and stir until dissolved. Add the Simple Syrup and stir until combined.

Makes approximately 2 quarts

1 pound fresh ginger, washed and unpeeled (makes approximately 2 cups ginger juice)

2 cups sugar

2 cups Simple Syrup (page 199)

VERMUT

DO-IT-YOURSELF VERMOUTH

For Americans, vermouth is looked at as the lowly mixer you only wanted a splash of in your martini or Manhattan, but for Spaniards, it has always been a prized possession to be drunk on the rocks with an orange twist. Vermouth is so popular in Spain, they have a phrase for consuming it: to *fer un vermút* means literally "to do a vermouth"; but it has also come to simply mean "to have a drink." As they do at the century-old tapas bars of Spain, at our restaurant we make our own wine potion, pour it on tap, and give it a prime spot on the menu.

Of course, on a daily basis we get the question: "What *is* vermut?" and so it is our job to demystify it. Vermouth is quite easy to understand if you break it down: It is a fortified and aromatized wine. "Fortified" meaning stronger in alcohol (typically accomplished by adding brandy, a grape spirit), and "aromatized" meaning steeped with botanicals (usually herbs, fruits, spices, and roots)—almost like a cold tea. In other words, it is a stronger, more flavorful wine or a low-alcohol cocktail of sorts. Vermouth can range from bone dry to super sweet, and the best thing about it is that there are no rules. You can use anything or everything to flavor it.

At the restaurant, we opened with a *tinto*, or red vermouth, our tribute to the classic, bittersweet Spanish vermouth. We like to say it tastes like a low ABV Negroni. The more we served, the more people talked about it and the word got out. Then we decided to devote a second tap line to vermouth, developing a seasonal dry vermouth using famers' market fruits and herbs with seasonal spices. Since then, we've made white versions we call Summer and Spring or Fall and Winter, as well as a spring rosé vermouth.

Making vermouth is way easier than you think; all you need are sherry and wine, aromatics and botanicals—those herbs, fruits, spices, and roots of your choosing. We got lucky, and have an amazing Indian grocer down the block who carries a wide array of crazy herbs and spices, but if you can't find a grocer like that, you can order a lot of these ingredients online (and can probably find many at a supermarket like Whole Foods or your local co-op or natural foods store). Because we're dealing with small amounts, these recipes use grams. Don't worry; your scale should show grams alongside ounces.

The key is to not be intimidated! For the wines in this recipe, just walk into your local wine and liquor store and ask for their cheapest amontillado-style sherry for our red vermouth, and fino style for our white vermouth. We use the brand Barbadillo for both, but any brand will work. When you do it right, you may never want to buy another bottle from the liquor store again.

BLANCO

HOMEMADE WHITE VERMOUTH

While their red counterpart was concocted to be drunk all year round, these white renditions were created seasonally, utilizing ingredients we picked up from the farmers' market or thought were right for the weather. We make one for the colder months and one for the warmer months. We wanted to share both recipes.

For either recipe, pour the sherry, wine, and honey into a large plastic container. Add the fruit. Wrap all the spices, roots, and leaves, and flowers in a large piece of cheesecloth (if you don't have cheesecloth, you can simply add the aromatics straight into the batch), tie it closed tightly with kitchen string, and put it into the liquid. Refrigerate for 3 days.

Strain through a fine-mesh strainer. Bottle the finished product in 1-quart mason jars and store in the fridge. Your vermouth will last up to a month.

To serve, pour over ice into a rocks glass and garnish with a lemon peel, or use in one of the following cocktail recipes.

Each makes about 3 quarts

Fall and Winter White Vermouth

3	750 ml bottles fino sherry
1½	cups Verdello or other juicy white wine
½	cup honey
3	apples, scrubbed but not peeled, cored and cut into large dice
1½	Asian pears, scrubbed but not peeled, cored and cut into large dice
2½	g cardamom pods
1	g whole cloves
5½	g dried marigold
5	g dried mace
3	chirotha sticks, muddled
4	cinnamon sticks
8	g peeled and finely chopped fresh ginger

Spring and Summer White Vermouth

3	750 ml bottles fino sherry
1½	cups white grenache or juicy white wine
¾	cup plus 2 tablespoons honey
½	pink grapefruit, diced
4	nasturtium flowers
1	g nasturtium leaves
8	g fresh chamomile flowers
3	g fresh green sorrel
½	g fresh lime basil
1¼	g rose bud
2½	g dried chamomile flowers
¼	g gentian root
¼	g lemon balm

TiNTo

HOMEMADE RED VERMOUTH

Believe it or not, from day one, our Tinto Vermouth has been one of the most widely ordered drinks at our restaurant. While the preparations may not be the most expedient—for this recipe you will need a kitchen scale and cheesecloth— once you have it bottled it up, we promise it will go down the fastest. This simple drink became so craveable that we'd pour it into a jar in order to bring some home to enjoy after a long shift.

Pour the sherry, wine, and pomegranate molasses into a large plastic container. Add the citrus peels and kaffir lime leaves. Wrap all the spices, roots, and dried flowers in a large piece of cheesecloth (if you don't have cheesecloth, you can simply add the aromatics straight into the batch), tie it closed tightly with kitchen string, and put it into the liquid. Refrigerate for 3 days.

Strain the vermouth through a fine-mesh strainer. Bottle the finished product in 1-quart mason jars and store in the fridge. Your homemade vermouth will last in the refrigerator for up to 1 month.

To serve, pour over ice in a rocks glass and garnish with an orange peel, or use in one of the following cocktail recipes.

Makes about 3 quarts

3	750 ml bottles amontillado sherry
1½	cups Tempranillo or any juicy red wine
¼	cup pomegranate molasses
	Peel of 1 lemon
	Peel of 1 orange
	Peel of ½ grapefruit
4	kaffir lime leaves
2	g freshly grated nutmeg
2	cinnamon sticks
3.6	g angelica root
5	g dried chamomile flowers
½	g gentian root

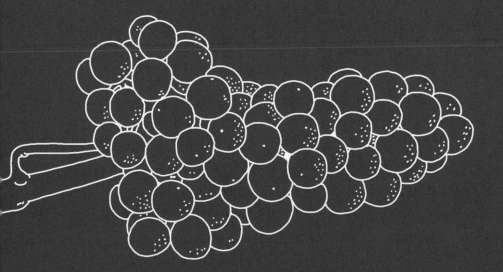

VERMOUTH COCKTAILS

While the Spanish drink vermouth straight, New York is a cocktail-crazy city, so we mix it up, literally. The best part about making your own vermouth is that it makes damn good cocktails, especially the classics. Homemade vermouth will make all the difference, but you can always go to your local wine store and ask for a good Spanish vermouth like Casa Mariol or Primativo Quiles; more and more shops are carrying them these days. If you can't find Spanish, go Italian; each recipe will denote whether you need the sweet or dry kind.

Gin Fizz

This style of classic cocktail is defined by its use of spirit (usually gin), citrus juice, (always lemon or lime), and carbonated water, hence the name "fizz." Since its creation, the fizz has evolved, and for us, a fizz is not a fizz without egg whites and vermouth. Given its lofty, pillowy presentation, this cocktail is impossible to miss when it hits the bar.

Combine all of the ingredients except the soda water and ice in a dry cocktail shaker and shake for 10 seconds. Add 2 ice cubes and shake again until the ice is dissolved. Rinse a Collins glass with absinthe, if using. Pour the drink into a Collins glass, add 2 fresh ice cubes, and top with the soda. Serve.

NOTE: *If you are ambitious, freeze the cocktail for 5 minutes in the glass, and pour soda very slowly to elevate the egg whites above the glass. It gives it a really dramatic effect.*

1½   oz Xoriguer Mahon gin, or any floral gin of your choosing (nothing too dry)

1   oz Fall White Vermouth (page 202) or dry vermouth of your choosing

½   oz Orange Syrup (page 196)

½   oz fresh lemon juice

1   egg white

2   oz soda water

Ice

Optional: absinthe rinse

Spritz

A "spritz" cocktail is the most classic *aperitivo*-style cocktail. *Aperitivo* is derived from the Latin verb *aperire*, which translates roughly as "to open up." These drinks are meant to open one's appetite, to open a meal, to open a conversation, a party, or whatever else you'd like to open up. We always like to open up with vermouth, because it is bitter and dry and gets your mouth watering. For those that don't feel comfortable drinking vermouth on its own, we add sparkling wine, Aperol, soda, and an orange and call it a "spritz." It's a gateway to straight vermouth, and bar none the best damn way to consume vermouth on a hot summer day.

Pour the vermouth and Aperol into a wineglass. Add ice, then top with the sparkling wine and soda water. Garnish with the orange slice and serve.

2½   oz Red Vermouth (page 203), or any sweet vermouth

¾   oz Aperol

Ice

2   oz cava, prosecco, or any sparkling white wine

1   oz soda water

Orange slice for garnish

Optional: orange bitters

NEGRONI

Invented by Italian Count Camillo Negroni in 1919, when he asked a bartender to spike his Americano cocktail (sweet vermouth and Campari) with gin, the Negroni cocktail is the perfect vehicle to show off your own Tinto Vermouth. In New York City, this has become the stirred cocktail of choice—wonderfully bittersweet, and easily drinkable—one that ten years ago no one would have thought to order. In the boozy cocktail category, this one drinks best in warmer months. For the colder months, substitute whiskey for gin, to make one of our all time favorite cocktails named the Boulevardier (see Note).

Pour the gin, vermouth, and Campari into a mixing glass. Add ice and stir for 15 revolutions. Strain over fresh ice into a rocks glass. Garnish with the orange twist and serve.

NOTE: *For a Boulevardier, substitute 1¼ oz Michter's Bourbon, or any bourbon of your choice, for the gin and cut the vermouth and Campari to ¾ oz each.*

1   oz gin (we use Barr Hill from Vermont, because it is distilled with local honey and balances our vermouth wonderfully. If you can't find it, use Plymouth, the best overall gin for Negronis)

1   oz Red Vermouth (page 203) or any sweet vermouth

1   oz Campari

    Ice

    Orange twist for garnish

SAN SEBASTIÁN

The San Sebastián, named after our home-base city in the Basque Country, was concocted to be our signature cocktail. It was the first cocktail we nailed, and it is the only cocktail that will never be removed from the list. This light stirred and boozy cocktail can be drunk all year round. We think it's what would happen if you substituted barrel-aged gin for whiskey in a Manhattan, then it fell in love with an Old-Fashioned and had a kid named Sazerac.

Pour all of the ingredients except the ice and garnishes into a mixing glass. Add ice and stir for 15 revolutions. Strain into a chilled rocks glass, add 1 big ice cube, and garnish with the Luxardo cherry and orange twist. Serve.

1   oz NY Distilling Chief Gowanus barrel-aged gin, or any other barrel-aged gin

¼   oz Spanish brandy

¼   oz Calvados

¾   oz sweet white vermouth

½   oz Red Vermouth (page 203) or red vermouth of your choosing

2   dashes Bittermans Boston bitters, or any light scented bitters of your choosing

1   dash Do Ferreiro Liquor de Herbas, absinthe, or other herbal liqueur of your choosing

     Ice

     Luxardo cherry for garnish

     Orange twist for garnish

SHERRY COCKTAILS

We really love sherry. This strange, unique, aged forti-fied wine from Andalucía, specifically Jerez, is one of the most versatile beverages in the world. The two main styles of sherry—fino, the light style, and oloroso, the oxidized, darker style—range from bone dry to super sweet and everything in between. Sherry is delicious on its own: it is salty, dry, and nutty, and there is nothing else like it. The wide-ranging flavors of sherry have also made it a phenomenal candidate for mixing and shaking with spirits and juices to create cocktails. Sherry was found in classic cocktails dating all the way back to the nineteenth century, and today the fortified wine is back in vogue—and has certainly become a close friend to many an NYC bartender.

SHERRY COBBLER

The Sherry Cobbler was always a fitting drink for us, for so many reasons. One, it embodies the idea of new Spanish: it is a classic American cocktail popularized in nineteenth century, and uses sherry, one of the most popular alcoholic beverages from Spain. Two, you can use whatever fruit you want, so it can change with the seasons. And, last but not least, it tastes just as good if not better out of a slushie machine.

    If you don't have time to make the syrup, just muddle a handful of fresh berries with 1 tablespoon sugar.

Combine the sherries and syrup in a cocktail shaker. Shake vigorously for 10 seconds with ice, then pour the contents into a rocks glass (or in bartender speak: "pour dirty," meaning pour without straining). Garnish with the mint sprig and cherry and serve.

1½ oz oloroso sherry

1½ oz fino sherry

¾ oz Berry/Sherry Syrup (recipe follows)

Small fresh mint sprig

Ice

Luxardo cherry

BERRY/SHERRY SYRUP

Combine all of the ingredients in a saucepan over medium-high heat and bring to a boil. Reduce the heat to medium-low and simmer gently until the berries' juices have been fully extracted, about 20 minutes. Strain through a fine-mesh strainer to remove the seeds, and store in glass, quart-sized jars in the refrigerator, where the syrup will keep for at least a week.

Makes 1 quart

½ pint blueberries

½ pint blackberries

2½ cups fino sherry

1½ cups sugar

Zest of ½ lemon

1½ teaspoons citric acid

½ cup water

BAMBOO

Traveling over the Pacific Ocean from Japan in the early 1900s, the Bamboo became so popular, it was sold in premixed bottles across America. Being equal parts sherry and vermouth, two fortified wines you know we love, and stirred up like a Manhattan, it was a no-brainer for us to show off at the bar.

Combine all of the ingredients except the ice and garnish in a mixing glass. Add ice and stir until chilled. Strain into a chilled coupe glass. Squeeze the oil from the lemon peel into the glass, drop it in, and serve.

1½ oz fino sherry

1½ oz Summer or Fall White Vermouth (page 202) or dry vermouth of your choosing

1 teaspoon cane syrup (recipe follows)

2 dashes Angostura bitters

2 dashes orange bitters

Ice

Lemon twist for garnish

CANE SYRUP

Combine the sugar and water in a saucepan and heat gently over medium heat, stirring occasionally to help dissolve the sugar. When the sugar is dissolved, about 5 minutes, remove from the heat and let cool. Store in an airtight container in the refrigerator for up to 1 month.

Makes about 2 cups

2 cups sugar

1 cup water

La Reina

La Reina translates to "the queen," and when this cocktail hit the menu, it was very much that. A refreshing, herbaceous, lemony spring and summer cocktail, La Reina quickly became our best-selling cocktail. It was one that we surely didn't want to leave out of this book, so you can impress all your friends at home.

Combine all the ingredients except the soda water and garnish in a cocktail shaker and shake for 10 seconds. Strain into a Collins glass, add fresh ice, and top with the soda. Garnish with the fresh herbs and the lemon twist and serve.

1½   oz gin (we like Greenhook for this one)

½   oz manzanilla or any dry sherry

½   oz Herb Syrup (recipe follows)

½   oz fresh lemon juice

½   oz Green Chartreuse

Ice

2   oz soda water

Lemon thyme or rosemary for garnish

Lemon twist for garnish

Herb Syrup

Put all the ingredients in a pot and bring to a boil over high heat. Once boiling, turn the heat down and simmer for 15 minutes, stirring occasionally. Take off the heat and let cool. Strain when cooled and store in the refrigerator; it will last for up to 2 weeks.

Makes 1 quart

1   cup water

1   cup sugar

5   sprigs fresh rosemary

5   fresh sage leaves

4   sprigs fresh lemon thyme

GiN & ToNiC

The gin and tonic, or as the Spanish call it more simply, the "GinTonic," is the undisputed king of cocktails in Spain. In fact, it has been coined the National Drink of Spain, and they have cocktail bars solely devoted to it. While there are some hypotheses as to why—the boom in good domestic gin producers, that it pairs best with the year-round temperate climate, that there is a large British influence in Spain and access to great tonics—it is undeniable that the Spanish are obsessed with this simple highball drink. And, after we traveled to Spain and saw it firsthand, we became obsessed, too.

A GinTonic is exactly what it sounds like: a mix of gin and tonic water (a bittersweet soda, the defining ingredient being quinine) poured over ice and always garnished with something to boost the flavor. But the Spaniards showed the world that the gin and tonic possibilities are endless. In Spain, it is a playful drink made with infinite combinations of gins, tonic waters, and garnishes.

The moment we got our liquor license, we knew we needed to pay homage to the Spanish GinTonic infatuation. We wanted to create one recipe, and do it exactly right. Since there are only three ingredients—the gin, the tonic, and the garnish had to dance in unison. We knew we wanted to use a local gin, and settled on Dorothy Parker Gin from New York Distilling Company, based in Brooklyn. Once we decided on that, we set out to nail the tonic syrup. Tonic syrup is a fickle thing. It needs to be bitter but not too bitter; sweet but not too sweet; and use just the right amount of cinchona bark (the root that gives it the all-important quinine).

After seemingly hundreds of trials, tribulations, and trips to the Indian grocer, we created the tonic syrup we wanted, one that when mixed with soda and gin, became bright, balanced, and downright crushable. To keep it simple, we garnished it with a lime wedge and lemon peel. For consistency and cachet, we decided to pour our G&T on tap; but at home, it's just as perfect with the right proportions of each ingredient. After all that, today, anytime you step foot into our restaurant, you can get a house GinTonic poured out of a draught, perfectly fizzy and addictive in every way we wanted it to be.

Pour the gin and tonic syrup into a Collins glass stir until mixed. Add ice, top with the soda water, and stir again. Squeeze the oil from the lemon peel into the glass and drop it in. Garnish with the lime wedge and serve.

1¾ oz Dorothy Parker Gin, or any gin of your choosing

½ oz Tonic Syrup (page 214)

Ice

3 ounces soda water

1 lemon twist

1 lime wedge

GIN TONIC

Tonic Syrup

You'll need a scale to measure the small amounts of spices here; grams will appear on most scales alongside the ounces. Combine the water, sugar, and cinchona bark in a large saucepan and bring to a boil over high heat. Reduce the heat to maintain a simmer and cook, stirring until the sugar is dissolved. Pour the syrup into a large heatproof container and add all of the remaining ingredients while the syrup is still hot. Let the syrup steep, covered, until cool. Refrigerate for 3 days. To bottle the finished product, strain through coffee filters into 1-quart mason jars. Store in the refrigerator for up to 1 month. **Makes about 2 quarts**

2 QUARTS WATER

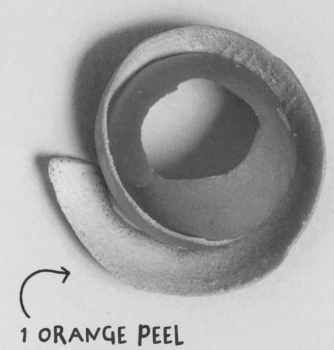

1 ORANGE PEEL

20 g CINCHONA BARK

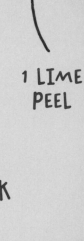

1 LIME PEEL

5 g LAVENDER

2 g GREEN CARDAMOM

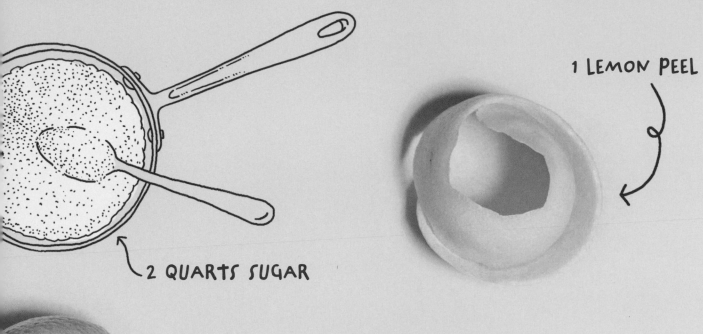

2 QUARTS SUGAR

1 LEMON PEEL

1 g ALLSPICE

1 g CHAMOMILE

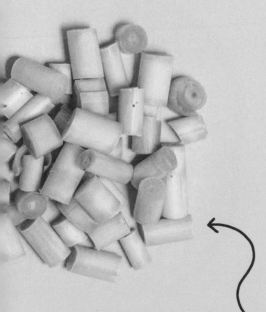

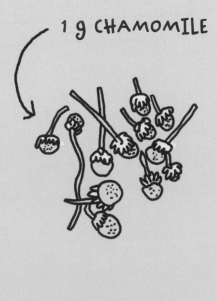

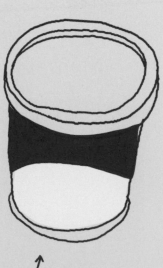

1 TBSP CITRIC ACID

4 STALKS OF
LEMONGRASS, CHOPPED

BOTELLÓN

CROQUETAS DE PATO
28

BASQUE DOGS
144

ARROZ AL CHINO
106

CHURROS CON CHOCOLATE
178

BEVERAGE PAIRING
REFRESCOS

In cities all across Spain, people party in the streets. *Botellón,* as they call it, has become the preferred way to pregame before going out to bars and clubs. With this dinner party, we've paid homage to the plaza parties in Spain, pairing the best greasy street food like croquetas and *bocadillos* (sandwiches) with the drinks so easy to prepare and share you can do so in a two-liter soda bottle. This party is best for better weather, and a backyard, where you can mix red wine and cola to make Kalimotxo (page 194), vermouth and citrus soda to make Tinto de Verano (page 197), sherry and ginger beer to make Rebujito (page 200), and sparkling wine and orange soda to make Agua de Valencia (page 196)—pack all the liter bottles in a big cooler to be served over ice with grilled hot dogs.

INDEx

THANK YOU

JM + NA

When dreaming of opening a restaurant, one thinks about the food and the drinks, about how the place will look, the style of service to be implemented, and perhaps about the sorts of folks who will become guests. What is harder to predict is the energy that a restaurant will create, and in the end, there may be no variable more important than the way a place makes you feel. This is what brings people back time and again, and for that positive energy we have our staff to thank.

So here's to our team: Rachel and Jessica for leading with style and grace; Jenni and the handful of other sous-chefs who helped create many of the recipes in this book; our cooks for bringing this food to life everyday; our bartenders for helping to create the beverages in this book and shaking and stirring them every night; our servers for throwing a neverending dinner party; our hosts for making everyone smile; and our porters for keeping our minds and spaces clean.

To those people who made this book possible: first and foremost to our artists who made this book pop and the process so much fun: Phil Wong for his endless design skills; Hugo Yoshikawa for being the most talented illustrator we know; and Ramsay de Give for his positive energy and eye behind the lens. To Sarah Smith, our unwavering agent; Meg Reid, whose idea it was for us to write a cookbook; and the team at Kyle Books, specifically our tireless editor Chris Steighner for giving us the chance to make it happen.

NA

To my parents, Dennis and Robin, for their unrelenting support. For bringing me up in a home that always smelled good and for showing me that going out to dinner is always a special event. To my brothers, Garrett and Drew, for being my closest friends and always pushing me to follow my passions. To my grandparents, Eric and Edith, Gertrude and Hy, for instilling in me that New York City entrepreneurial hustle. To anyone who has ever taken a chance on me and believed I could do more: to Rachel Jackson, who gives me endless chances, and pushes me harder than anyone else; to Professor Eric Clemons, who spurred an independent study and is the reason I am in hospitality; to Joel Steiger, my first and only real boss; to Andrew Tarlow, David Swinghamer, and David Steele for providing continued mentorship and inspiration.

JM

To my parents, Ben and Jan, for encouraging my love of cooking and dream of opening a restaurant, and for moving to New York together after college—a city that fueled my desire to always eat well and allowed me to attack my goals starting at a tender age. To my sister, Rebecca, for challenging me, among other ways, by becoming a vegetarian. To Marina, my favorite dinner companion for thirteen years and counting, my biggest critic (everyone needs one), and now my wife and an incomparable mother—watching you with Nina has taken my admiration and appreciation of you to uncharted levels. There's no one I'd rather cook for.

Design by
Phil Wong

Illustration by
Hugo Yoshikawa

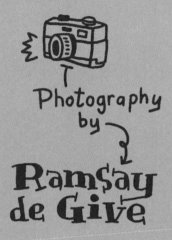

Photography by
Ramsay de Give

Philip Wong is a designer from New York City working in fashion and product development—he probably designed the T-shirt you're wearing. He once ate twenty pintxos in one sitting.

Hugo Yoshikawa is a French-Japanese illustrator now working in London. He grew up traveling, living in Tokyo, Paris, New York, and Bangkok. He loves drawing and cooking as they don't have a language per se and can be appreciated universally. Influenced by Franco-Belgian comics and architecture through his travels, he makes line-based drawings of everyday life with a touch of Tintin.

Ramsay de Give is a photographer by trade, farmer by heart. He grew up in Santa Fe, New Mexico, and holds a strong appreciation for spicy food and early morning light.

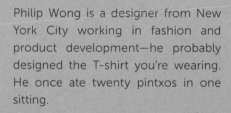

Nate ADLER

As a native New Yorker, Nate Adler was fascinated by the restaurant world from the start. During his years at the University of Pennsylvania, he launched a delivery and take-out food concept serving "home-cooked meals" to college students. After graduation, he landed his first real job at Danny Meyer's Blue Smoke, then working his way up from server assistant to beverage director. In 2014, he teamed up with Miller to open Huertas restaurant, running the front of house and shaping the beverage menu. As preparation, Adler traveled in Spain to immerse himself in the country's drinking culture and become an expert in its traditions. In 2018 Adler is opening his second restaurant, Gertie, an all-day spot serving up New York comfort food in Brooklyn.

Jonah MILLER

Jonah Miller was drawn to cooking at a young age and began his career as a fourteen-year-old summer intern in the kitchen of the legendary New York restaurant Chanterelle. During high school, he spent summers working at Gramercy Tavern and Savoy. While in college at New York University, he studied abroad in Madrid, living on the iconic Calle de las Huertas and eating up everything Spain had to offer. After three impactful years in the kitchen at Danny Meyer's Maialino, ready to strike out on his own, he traveled back to Spain to put the finishing touches on his vision for a restaurant named Huertas. The primary subject of the nonfiction book *Generation Chef,* Miller was nominated for the Rising Star award by the James Beard Foundation and has been named to both the Zagat and Forbes 30 under 30 lists.